This series offers the concerned reader basic guidelines and *practical* applications of religion for today's world. Although decidedly Christian in focus and emphasis, the series embraces all denominations and modes of Bible-based belief relevant to our lives today. All volumes in the Steeple series are originals, freshly written to provide a fresh perspective on current—and yet timeless—human dilemmas. This is a series for our times. Among the books:

How to Read the Bible
James Fischer

How to Live Your Faith
L. Perry Wilbur

A Spiritual Handbook for Women
Dandi Daley Knorr

Temptation: How Christians Can Deal with It
Frances Carroll

With God on Your Side: A Guide to Finding Self-Worth Through Total Faith
Doug Manning

A Daily Key for Today's Christians: 365 Key Texts of the New Testament
William E. Bowles

Walking in the Garden: Inner Peace from the Flowers of God
Paula Connor

How to Bring Up Children in the Catholic Faith
Carol and David Powell

Sex in the Bible: An Introduction to What the Scriptures Teach Us About Sexuality
Michael R. Cosby

How to Talk with God Every Day of the Year: A Book of Devotions for Twelve Positive Months
Frances Hunter

God's Conditions for Prosperity: How to Earn the Rewards of Christian Living
Charles Hunter

Pilgrimages: A Guide to the Holy Places of Europe for Today's Traveler
Paul Lambourne Higgins

Journey into the Light: Lessons of Pain and Joy to Renew Your Energy and Strengthen Your Faith
Dorris Blough Murdock

Frances L. Carroll

FRUSTRATION

how Christians can deal with it

A SPECTRUM BOOK

Prentice-Hall, Inc.
Englewood Cliffs, New Jersey 07632

Library of Congress Cataloging in Publication Data

Carroll, Frances L.
    Frustration: how Christians can deal with it.

    (Steeple books)
    "A Spectrum Book."
    Includes index.
        1. Frustration.   2. Christian life—1960-
    I. Title.   II. Series.
    BF575.F7C37   1984   248.4   83-19110
    ISBN 0-13-330812-X
    ISBN 0-13-330804-9 (pbk.)

*For my special second mom,
my mother-in-law, Mary D. Carroll;
and her son, my husband, Sandy.*

1 2 3 4 5 6 7 8 9 10

ISBN 0-13-330812-X

ISBN 0-13-330804-9 {PBK.}

Prentice-Hall International, Inc., *London*
Prentice-Hall of Australia Pty. Limited, *Sydney*
Prentice-Hall Canada Inc., *Toronto*
Prentice-Hall of India Private Limited, *New Delhi*
Prentice-Hall of Japan, Inc., *Tokyo*
Prentice-Hall of Southeast Asia Pte. Ltd., *Singapore*
Whitehall Books Limited, *Wellington, New Zealand*
Editora Prentice-Hall do Brasil Ltda., *Rio de Janeiro*

contents

preface

This book is about us. It is as timely as today and as futuristic as tomorrow. In it we cover the problems and heartaches associated with frustration. We determine the causes, examine our attitudes, and then learn the solution to the problem of frustration in our lives.

Frustration enters into each of our lives no matter who we are or where we live. We cannot escape it, for it is a human emotion. For the Christian man or woman there is no need to allow frustration to bind him or her down and render his or her life useless. Using the Bible as our chief resource, we will learn how to deal with life's frustrations through the power of Christ in our lives.

Acknowledgments

Each part of this book is of equal importance and we are grateful to those who have supported our efforts. Grateful appreciation and acknowledgment is given to the following:

The New King James Version (NKJV), ©1979, 1980, 1982, Thomas Nelson Publishers, Inc.

The Williams New Testament, ©1937, 1965, 1966, by Edith Williams. Used by permission of Moody Press, Moody Bible Institute of Chicago.

The New American Standard Bible (NAS), ©The Lockman Foundation 1960, 1962, 1963, 1968, 1971, 1972, 1973, 1975, 1977.

Webster's New Twentieth Century Dictionary, ©1979 by Simon and Schuster.

Quote-Unquote, compiled by Lloyd Cory, ©1977 by Victor Books, SP Publications.

It would be impossible, without their support, to write a book of this sort. The Word of God is an important resource and with their permission I have quoted from these sources.

chapter
1

thinking about frustration

Each of us has an optimal stress level. To keep stress from becoming distress, we must have not only the right amount but the right kind for the right duration. Distress often results from prolonged or unvaried stress, or from frustration.

Webster's dictionary gives us a clear view of what we may encounter as frustration enters our lives: "Frustrate—to make null; to nullify; to bring to nothing; to render of no effect." Frustration enters in ever so casually and slowly begins to spin its web of trouble and deceit. Frustration, like a black widow spider, seems determined to entrap its victim. Once trapped, the victim is rendered inoperable, thus allowing the aggressor to complete its task.

Although this illustration may seem dramatic, we must begin to realize what frustration's intentions are. It seeks to bind us. Frustration forces us to consider a series of negative thoughts and actions. It can cause the spiritual qualities and strongholds we possess to fade into the background unless we control it. It projects attitudes of worthlessness. The "blahs" tend to set in. Due to the resulting frustration, we may face numerous attacks by the adversary, which will seek to dampen our spiritual life. To master the feelings of depression, worry, anxiety, emptiness, lifelessness, and rejection will take discipline on our part. We will have to subdue frustration's attack, so that we will achieve victory over it.

Before we engage the enemy of frustration, we must understand it. Often those engaged in dealing with it are unaware of the cause of their dilemma. Our approach will be to use a common-sense reasoning and biblical understanding of the spiritual warfare to overcome frustration. Frustration, like the flu, usually strikes its victims quickly, often without the slightest warning. Its victims wonder, "What is happening to me? Where did this feeling come from? Why now? Why do I feel this way?" Our need is to have a certain knowledge of the source and then treat it accordingly. There is always a cure for frustration. We just need to seek it.

Sometimes the victims of "frustration flu" seem incapable of treating it. Their lack of training and knowledge on the subject makes it a hazard to their spiritual welfare. Our treatment of the "frustration flu" will be to examine it in God's Word for all ages, the Holy Bible. This will guide us to vital information on the subject as well as give us the cure to the frustration flu when it comes our way. There is no greater spiritual medicine than the pure Word of God. And the cure is lasting.

Why Are We a Frustrated People?

The subject of frustration is fascinating. Like you, I have had periods in my life when I wrestled with frustration. I wondered why I never found answers to the problem. Since I began this study God has revealed new insights on the subject to me. God has given me a burden to share my findings. Recall, I am not a consultant or a professional, only a special friend through Christ. My solutions are found in part by experience but mainly in application of God's Word to my life.

My many experiences with frustration have been painful for me. Because of them I was forced to consider the reasons I allowed frustration to overpower me. Even more distressing, I was constrained to seek after the cure and apply it to my life. I discovered that it is necessary to come to a positive realization that most frustrations are brought about by our own attitudes. God knows our need to understand frustration. I offer to you the things I have learned through reading the Scriptures, prayer, and meditation with the Holy Spirit. I believe they will be useful to you in overpowering frustration.

At times we find ourselves frustrated because of attitudes and situations that seem beyond our control. The realization that we cannot always have our own way or change situations can cause problems. We feel a certain amount of injustice is done us in that life would be better if this or that matter could be done away with.

Another reason for frustration is the world situation. Life has progressed so rapidly that we can scarcely keep pace with it. Consider the changes that have occurred in technology within the last 20 to 30 years. My thoughts drift back a few years. There were no fast-food restaurants. Ice cream was usually found in drugstores that contained small soda fountains and possibly a jukebox. In my hometown, Memphis, they had only begun the interstate highway system. The jet plane was uncommon and, when one broke the sound barrier, shaking the window frames, we were amazed. Television was just in its infancy. We have advanced ever so rapidly!

When television was a "baby," our viewing was limited in part by the small screen, sparse programming, poor reception, and, of course, the radio, which was still a competitor. Little did we realize what lay ahead of us. Television has changed the world. We have expanded our horizons and gained new knowledge through it.

No wonder frustration is at such a high point today! Look at the things we must contend with. Our society has been transformed into large communities and cities instead of many small towns and rural areas. While seeking to conform to the standards and technological advances of today, we have often pushed our spiritual standards into the background. We no longer focus our attention on the family. Now there is a growing list of things and purposes that demand our attention. We live life in the fast lane to gain pleasure and happiness.

We have many conveniences to make us happy, and yet there seems to be little happiness among us. If our spiritual needs and development have not progressed as rapidly as the development of today's technology, then we face numerous problems. Frustration is easily found today. Often we need only look in the mirror to find it staring us in the face.

One of life's greatest frustrations comes through the desire to "keep up with the Joneses." God love the Joneses, their struggle is to keep up with the Johnsons ... and on and on it goes! Frustration is frequently found because we will not or cannot be content with what we have. We are always looking beyond what we have to what we think we want. Do you see how this can further frustrate you? The mind says, "If we have a better home or a job which pays more, a child to make our home complete, nicer clothes, or a certain amount of money in the bank, then life would be complete and perfect." We battle with self-centeredness each day.

Dear friends, we must focus on our blessings instead of our desires. When turned to obsession, these desires turn us from God. This causes us to focus on selfish things. And this causes us to be self-centered. Many of life's frustrations could be avoided by setting proper priorities. We must select the right perspective and then follow through with it. God's plan for us shows us the way to achieve this success. Through it we will gain peace and happiness.

Frustration's Effects

Frustration places strange ideas in our mind and spirit. If we give it free reign, we may encounter many problems that arise from a negative attitude. Let's look at some of the areas in which frustration can alter our mental, spiritual, and physical well-being. Bear in mind that frustrations can be turned around to help us achieve a happier life. That's what our study is all about.

MENTAL ATTITUDES

Frustration quietly slithers into our thought processes. As it does, our outlook becomes slightly altered. We begin to lose our grip on many situations. Common-sense attitudes no longer prevail. The things that were once unimportant now seem to become life's driving force. The problem that once seemed small and insignificant now becomes a raging monster. That thorn in the flesh has festered and swollen. Frustration has almost gained control of our mental attitude, and we feel downtrodden. We might even experience extreme changes in our attitudes and actions, because we feel separated from reality. We need a definite change in attitude.

Consider how our minds are affected by our self-centered reactions. We focus on the problem in a negative mood. Our common sense says, "We need to rid ourselves of this problem." But instead we allow it to grow stronger each moment. This is what frustration does best; it makes little problems larger rather than eliminate them. As our anguish, anger, depression, and anxiety begin to surface, we feel we need to vent our emotions and let go. Flare-ups become common occurrences. Our attitudes and emotions run deep. In our efforts to express our displeasures in life we sometimes lose control of our better judgment.

Although we feel we cannot overcome our feelings of anguish and anxiety, however, *all is not hopeless!* We can regain our composure when we understand what steps to take. As we will soon learn, for the Christian, frustration is overcome through Christ's strength, not one's own. The negative forces in our lives are set aside by the powers of the Holy Spirit. Our lives are what we allow the Holy Spirit to make them! Christ in us gives us the assurance that joy, not misery, can be our mental attitude at all times. Remember, our study is to show the victory not the defeat that we Christians can have over frustration.

When I was a young girl I heard my mother say, "Mrs. B____ is happiest when she is the most miserable." Sadly, there are many people who seem to be the happiest when they have something negative to dwell on. The more negative the cause, the more they enjoy it. This is an attitude that, I feel, displeases God. We are to be content and happy in our faith. Always look for the good that comes through knowing Christ. Negative actions accomplish very little. They only place our focus on things that are unspiritual and unhappy.

Allow me to share some examples of wrong attitudes I have had to learn in my life. My past is filled with plenty of examples of what not to be more than what to be in a given situation. Perhaps this is the most valid reason of all for me to share my life with you. Hopefully, you might avoid the pitfalls that brought me great mental suffering and anguish.

Throughout most of my life there pervaded a negative attitude and feeling of "no self-worth." I never felt "good" about life nor even liked myself much. Somehow I had learned a wrong set of standards. I learned the power of negative thinking. Thinking negatively helps us discover our dark side. It forms a cloud of gloom and despair that fills the spirit and weakens our trust. I became a master at hiding my emotions. I often concealed my true feelings from those about me. Consequently, I hated life. I suppose I even hated myself. I was uncertain and uneasy in groups or crowds of people. I preferred the closeness of two or three friends for security. In my mind and heart there was a feeling that I was nothing and had nothing to offer anyone. My life was a hopeless mess. Everything I sought to do seemed to flop. I could barely cope. I played the game of being happy, while all along I was so miserable. I did not understand how to look for the good in life.

The powers of darkness were closing the doorway of peace and contentment. I often considered suicide. I dwelled on thoughts about the best way to do the dirty deed. I did not want to blunder any effort, so all had to go well. Countless hours were wasted thinking negative thoughts. Frustration gives us the opportunity either to better ourselves or to slip into a deeper well of despair. I found myself slipping. I would plead with God to do something to relieve my problems. I waited and waited for something to happen.

How gracious our God is to ignore many of our rash prayers. I could almost hear His voice whisper, "This is not the way to live. Jesus is the way!" Still I ignored the call God issued me and continued walking in my own self-pity and discontentment. I had not really understood what Christ had offered me through His love. If I had, I would have changed. I did not fully believe that Christ was concerned for me, and in my spiritual blindness I stumbled on looking for my own answers to frustrating problems.

At this stage in my life something else happened. I became very angry at God. I would find myself screaming at Him in anguish and torment, "If You really love me, why don't You do something for me? If You are, God, really are, then why don't You reveal Yourself to me?" I desperately wanted God to do something, anything, to relieve the torment, but I felt nothing.

Oh, what a sad time of life this was for me. Had I looked a little beyond myself, I would have recognized that help had already arrived. But I was so bound with spiritual frustration and mental anguish that I could see nothing other than my own needs. I had not come to realize that it is in giving our love to others that life finds meaning and is worth living. My focus was still entirely on myself. I really didn't care about anything else other than my own misery.

As you can imagine, my life was a mess—a disaster area containing nothing but broken pieces of a life gone sour. Frankly, I needed help. But none came. My mind was beset with anger, resentment, and frustration, and I still played the game of church along with everything else. I went through the steps of worship, but my heart was still empty and aching. While I continued to look the part of a Christian, I hated the church and resented the people. None of these people even said so much as, "Hello, I'm glad to see you today." I needed them to care. I wanted them to care.

My attitude toward people began to change for the worse. My spirit and heart hardened as I became hardened to the Word of God. To make the situation even worse, we had been ordered to go to Rota, Spain. Rota was the last place on earth I wanted to be. I was in torment the entire 18 months we were stationed there. Rota was my stumbling block; it caused me even greater frustration.

I hated living in Rota. In fact, the only thing I disliked worse than Rota was my husband, Sandy. I reasoned in my mind that all this was his fault. It was out of the question for us to get Navy housing because we didn't have children. Thus we were placed near the bottom of the list. No telephone, no television, one English-speaking radio station, and lots of sand added to the anger I felt. Each Sunday I went to church, sitting in the right side of the chapel, hoping, waiting for something to happen. My life was at an all-time low. I felt sure someone would speak to me, but no one did.

My life remained in this state of despair for several more years. After Rota we moved to a college town in the United States. Things didn't improve much. College towns are socially structured. Sandy worked in the Nuclear Science Center as a technician. We were not considered students, nor were we really faculty. Since Sandy did not have a degree, there was no opportunity to fit into the faculty social structure. The students thought of him as almost an old man. He didn't fit in anywhere. We were more or less misfits.

While living in this town, we attended church regularly. We didn't seem to get much response there either. (Allow me to mention, I am not pointing a guilty finger at anyone! The problem was ours as well as theirs. We should have tried to find a way to reach them as well.) We were, like others, just people passing through going to college. With the exception of a few Sunday School socials, no one sought to keep in contact with us to see if we had a need or wanted to be friends.

Christian people, we need to make a clear evaluation of where we stand in our commitment to helping others. We need to watch for opportunities to share our faith.

I guess it would be all right to say that I was unhappy in this place. I wanted a new start in life. I would beg God, as I cried and prayed, "Please let someone know I need a friend and that I hurt." But once again no help came. God was really testing me out, so that when the time was right I would respond to His call.

By the time we arrived in Arkansas in 1971 my spirit had become hard and almost unreachable. I was filled with distrust and anger. I ignored almost all Christian people. I had thought that people you wanted as friends or expected to be friends always let you down. I had become disappointed and disoriented.

Our mental attitude can make or break our spirit. When we become discouraged, we simply cannot achieve much. In fact we barely strive to run the race of life at all. We feel defeated and overpowered by our adversaries. This is, of course, not a healthy way to think, nor is it recommended. No, not ever! There is a way of victory through a deeper understanding of Christ's messages, and we need to learn it so that we may be Spirit-filled Christians.

With my life in a complete mess, there came a time for decision. What did I want in life? Where did I stand as a Christian? Was there a meaning to life or not? All these questions continued to whirl through my mind. It became clear it was evaluation time for Frances Carroll.

God taught me some important truths about myself as I reviewed my life. Some of these were:

1. I had forgotten how to love. That's wrong, sinful in fact.
2. I was very selfish and self-centered. That stung!
3. I had failed because I had not sought to overcome the negative side of life.
4. My life must change course or else! God knew what else!
5. Happiness was not mine because I had looked for it within myself. Happiness is in sharing and loving with others.
6. God really does love me!
7. Every breath I take and every thought I have are important to God.
8. God's son, Jesus Christ, died for me! He *really did*. I had never comprehended this before. Christ had to become personal to me.

9. My life had been lived to please my own selfish desires and pleasures. No one else was important. I was blind to the needs of others.
10. God had a better way of life for me. He wanted to change the let-down parts of my spirit and lift me up to give my life greater meaning.
11. Christ would and could show me the way to live a life filled with happiness and meaning. He could make me the person I wanted to be. He would show me how to love myself.
12. God taught me that I must throw away the hate I had for myself and others and replace it with growing love for others.
13. I must learn to walk with Christ and follow His way, not my own. He knew my needs and how to renew my spirit. I needed Jesus!

I would like to tell you that from that day onward things were fabulous, but they were not. Overcoming frustration takes time and effort. It takes time to rebuild the brokenness in our lives. The course is not easy to alter—it isn't supposed to be. There is a secret to this transformation of character, however. It is in allowing Christ to be the Lord of our lives.

Truly, it is Christ who makes the difference. Our mental attitude should be positive because Christ lives. It is Christ's love that sets us apart from the negative aspects in life. Christ stands with us as we journey through life, never leaving our side. We should renew our faith and trust in Jesus, allowing Him to teach us the proper attitudes. Without Christ we can do little; with Him the person we are can reach God's fullest potential for our lives. As a believer in Christ, we can have a special relationship with the Savior. My life is now filled with *His* joy and *His* gladness, because I feel secure in Him. The struggle to find myself ended when I discovered the hidden treasure of being in Christ.

SPIRITUAL ATTITUDES

It is imperative for the Christian to have a proper spiritual attitude. While some, seemingly, think little about spiritual matters, still others of us dwell on the spiritual all the while. A proper balance in our spiritual attitudes is necessary. As Christians, it is time for us to stop and set our spiritual priorities in order. Each of us has a wide range of views and reasoning, and each Christian must be encouraged to share his or her gifts.

Let us examine the idea that some Christians never seem to have a spiritual thought or to mature in faith. To this type of person the spiritual life isn't necessary at all, and they almost completely ignore it. They say, "I don't have time for all that religious junk. That's for sissies." They are often "supercool" in appearance. Within some of these people simmers a spirit that stews about everything and anything. They don't want "that religious junk," because they are afraid it may change some of their old attitudes. Some even enjoy doing wrong. They can't imagine how they could alter any habit they have to please anybody—let alone Jesus Christ. Very often these persons seek answers to their problems and come up empty time and time again. They lack directional faith. From outward appearances it's not easy to see their emotional needs, but they need guidance. Many of us have become masters at hiding our feelings and at playing games with others. But the need for Christ is real.

"Supercool" people are usually right in the middle of everything. They decide something needs to be done right now about a trouble-some situation but never have the right solution to the problem. They're so in tune with life that they cannot hear anything over the loud music. They argue about everything and achieve very little. Furthermore, they just want to do their own thing, which is almost completely 180 degrees out of God's will. They know life is not what it should be but just aren't sure they want to change. Although thoughts of the Lord have crossed their mind, they hesitate. They say, "No, not now. I'll accept You later." These individuals need to understand the words Jesus spoke in John 10:10, "I am come that they might have life, and that they might have it more abundantly."

The Spirit of Christianity. There are spiritual Christians and then again there are *spiritual* Christians. There is an ongoing struggle in the Christian community about how and what our spiritual condition should be. Surely this problem causes great frustration in the hearts of God's people. Our effort here will be to concentrate on the struggle that individuals encounter as they seek to live for Christ.

I suppose one of the most frustrating feelings Christians have is caused by the lack of understanding of unbelievers. They think, "Surely we aren't all that different from the rest of the world, are we?" The answer must be "Yes, we are!" The Scriptures instruct us not to conform to the standards and ideas of this world, for they will misdirect us.

To help us further in our understanding of spiritual values, let us look at some important passages of Scripture. Romans 12:2 (NAS) says, "And do not be conformed to this world, but be transformed by the renewing of your mind, that you may prove what the will of God is, that which is good and acceptable and perfect."

1. "Do not be conformed to this world." Christian, do not let the standards and attitudes of the world bend and twist your spirit until it is no longer recognizable. The Scriptures teach that the world is controlled by the spirit of darkness (Satan). Jesus Christ is the Light of our lives, the promised One sent from God. We are to be different from unbelievers in every manner. Be like Jesus, strive for perfection within yourself.

We are only passing through this world. We are sojourners along the road of life heading toward eternity with God. As we travel, we encounter certain adverse conditions. As Christians, we are to react properly toward these adversities. We should maintain a special calmness and peace of mind, because the Holy Spirit is in our lives. Do not be conformed; rather, stand firm! We carry a visible message to others regarding our faith. How we deliver it either gives someone the wrong understanding of Christ or the right impression—that believing *does* make a difference.

2. "Be transformed by the renewing of your mind." "How," you ask, "are we transformed by the renewing of our minds?" Well, it takes time and effort on our part. Consider that many of the feelings of frustration you encounter will disappear when you receive a fully renewed mind and regenerated spirit. You will be changed and glad for it.

To transform your mind as a Christian, you must rid yourself of wrong attitudes and thought patterns. Don't get scared! It isn't as difficult as it sounds. It just takes commitment to the task and giving the Lord some freedom to do His part. The hardest step to take is deciding to do it. Transformation comes when you evaluate your life as it is; determine what it is that is lacking; and seek to pursue a new attitude through Christ Jesus.

You see, we must look at our lives as Christ does, then we will desire to clean up the wrong attitudes that have been acquired over the years. By seeking God's will (His plan for our lives), we discover that God has placed us in a unique position—we have become children of God. We are adopted children, allowed to share the Good News of Christ.

When we allow transformation to take place, a few changes occur. Most of them are small and almost unnoticed, but others cause us to alter some of our old ways. Transformation is achieved through reading and studying the Scriptures, prayer, and commitment to the Lord Jesus. As transformation occurs, we may encounter moments of temptation, which cause us to struggle with our old will. In my book, *Temptation: How Christians Can Deal with It,* we take an honest look at what temptation seeks to do to us and learn how to overcome it. Remember, temptation, like frustration, is brought about by forces trying to turn us away from God. In our efforts to change the unlovely parts of our lives, both frustration and temptation may enter in, telling us, "There is no way in the world *you* can live by godly standards!" When this occurs, recall that *you* have the mind of Christ as a Christian, and you need not allow the negative forces in life to control your spiritual well-being.

3. "That you may prove what the will of God is." I have given much thought and prayer about the "will of God" and my life. Perhaps you, like I, have struggled with this phrase. How do we determine the will of God in our lives? How can I be certain that what I do is a part of God's will? My answer is that the will of God will be tried as we step forth in each new adventure.

Many of us do not know what the will of God is for our lives, because we are unable to discern the Spirit of God in our hearts. There is an inward conflict that seems to say, "Why should I do the will of God? Of what profit is it to seek God? How is it possible to know God's will in my life?" After wrestling with these questions, we often find that the only way to know God's perfect plan for our lives is *to know God personally.* We have to pray and then listen as God speaks to us. He instructs us on a one-to-one basis in His ways. He is a *personal* God!

The manner in which I learn the will of God is this: I pray and ask for guidance. I ask Him to reveal the things I need to know. I ask Him to close any doors that might lead me into wrongdoing. It is necessary to be sincere and to be sure that we want to be God's person—then we can be sure He will direct us. Step forth in faith and trust Him. Know God has your best interests at heart. As Christians, you and I are set aside to perform many important tasks to show others the way to Christ. We must first allow Him to show us the way each day.

Knowing God's will is not always easy but understanding that He will guide you is vital. Although He does not take control of your life, He is always available to you and will not allow you to fail in the mission before you. Never allow your mind or spirit to guide you into a belief which states any idea other than, "I am of value to God!" It is Christ that we center our beliefs on, not spirits or doctrines set by man.

The Struggle. Christians struggle with ideas and doctrines almost daily. Sometimes I get so frustrated listening to ministers and evangelists tell us, "We are not worthy enough to be Christians. We can never do anything good enough or pleasing enough to be called God's children." I am deeply grieved when I hear this idea tossed over the pulpit and cast so carelessly in our laps.

Consider this idea: while we know that we may not be worthy within our own power, Christ considered our lives of great value. If this were not so, He would never have given His life for our sins. Christ died for you! Christ died for me! We are special, because Christ has given His *all* for us. We are not rejects! Furthermore, Christ in His glory has given us a reason to live—to serve for and with Him throughout eternity. That makes us special because of Christ.

Christ uses people to change situations and life styles. He takes us, in our less-than-perfect state, and allows us to be a part of His ministry. We may be involved in a small ministry of helps by sharing words of encouragement, praying, teaching, comforting, or ever so many other tasks, but our Lord has a job for each of us to do. To say that we are not worthy is to tell Christ that we cannot be a good helper. I just don't think this is an effective way to approach the challenges that are before us. Therefore, let us press on for Christ.

Please know that while we are not perfect, we are forgiven. Rejoice and be glad, for He has assigned you tasks to perform in His Kingdom both here and in heaven. Find great joy in understanding that each challenge is sent from our Lord, who knows our capabilities, our limitations, and the depth of our commitment. Everything he sends us guides us into a deeper maturity and a stronger faith as we strive to do God's will. Although the results may not be as we would have them, they are acceptable to God! He knew what the outcome would be before you were called to such a task.

Am I worthy in God's sight? Yes, I am worthy! So are you! We are worthy because the Spirit of Christ dwells within the heart of those who have accepted Christ as Lord and Savior. We cannot allow frustration to take control of our life because of the judgment of another. The Lord Jesus Christ is our Guide throughout each day, and He knows our worth!

PHYSICAL FRUSTRATIONS

This area of study is one that is difficult for me to address. I must draw on the experiences of others. Certainly, there are many who could speak on this subject far better than I.

There are many forms of physical frustration. Today we see the handicapped making an active attempt to alter many of the physical barriers that frustrate them. It is difficult for most of us to comprehend their problems as they endeavor to achieve what is considered a normal life style.

There are thousands upon thousands of people who daily face physical frustrations. Perhaps their health has become a factor, and they are restricted in some manner. Physical limitations are not always easy to handle, but there are many people who have a special courage of their own. There are others who, just because their bodies slow down as years roll by, tend to become frustrated. Each of us should be sensitive to the physical or mental capabilities or limitations of others.

Because individuals are somehow limited does not mean their life is meaningless. In fact, their life might be fuller than yours or mine. It is important that our reactions and relationships to each individual are real. It is important how we communicate in the face of these problem areas, remembering that, even in limitation, the individual's life is of equal value to God. Many of life's handicaps are overcome by sheer determination and will and through God's guiding love. Let us not limit others because we do not understand. God expects each of us to be strong-hearted and do our best.

If you are a person who is physically limited, there are certain things to remember.

- God knows your situation and limitations.
- Frustration need not control your life style.
- Positive attitudes are important in dealing with your abilities.
- Your life can be an important example to others, no matter what your limitations.
- God has a purpose for your life as well as an opportunity for you to serve Him. Seek an understanding of God's will for you.

QUESTIONS
1. Make a list of six things that tend to frustrate you.

2. Why do these things bother you so often?

3. What do you seek to learn from this study on frustration?

4. How important is a good mental attitude in dealing with the frustrations of life?

5. Locate three Scriptures that encourage you to overcome these negative feelings.

6. How do emotions cause further frustrations?

7. Does frustration have to overpower your Christian life?

8. What steps can you take to avoid the recurrence of frustration in your daily life?

9. What part does unhappiness play in fostering frustration?

10. In a notebook, state briefly what the Christian life means to you personally.

11. What does Romans 12:2 mean to you?

12. How is transformation brought about in your Christian life?

13. What does the phrase "the will of God" refer to in the Christian life?

14. What are your greatest struggles at this moment in life?

chapter
2

who is frustrated?

> *When we are in high spirits, the world is a great place—your friends are the dearest, your kiddies the smartest, your employees the best, and your canary the tweetiest. But when your mood is dark, the world is bleak, your friends selfish, your children ungrateful, your boss the meanest, and even your pup, wagging his tail, is nothing but a big nuisance.*
>
> Sonja Eiteljorg

Views we hold and images we project are ever so important. How we see ourselves and how we project ourselves might be entirely different from how we actually are. We may seem to be cold and harsh, while all the while we are completely the opposite. This chapter is dedicated to our self-images, our projected images, and our true personalities.

Some of us almost seem to have split personalities, don't we? The image one person has of us might be quite different from the image another has of us. At times we pretend to be something we are not in order to cope with a situation. We may be hiding a secret hurt. We might be like a roaring lion at the office, whereas all the while be a quiet and shy person on the inside. Or we may seem to be a "cold fish" and uncaring, yet have a loving heart and a giving spirit. We often project images of ourselves that are impersonal or distant to avoid the pain and frustration accompanying personal relationships. We may feel unworthy of acceptance, so we throw up an invisible wall to protect ourselves.

It is well for us to remember as we study this chapter that, as Christians, the image we project is important. We may be someone's

special example of Christian living—good or bad! For us to see ourselves as God's children, as caring people, we must learn who we are
within ourselves. When we understand ourselves as others see us, then
we can overcome many of life's little frustrations. So then, let us press
on and look at our lives as living examples of the Christian life.

Who Am I?

Who am I? This is a striking question, isn't it? The sad fact is that many
of us simply do not know ourselves at all. We struggle within ourselves
to understand our actions and motives. It is not until we search our
hearts and know our spirits, as Christ knows us, that we can gain self-
respect. Knowing yourself, as a person, is very important.

For many years I was involved with a struggle that almost gained
control of my heart: I did not know myself. I struggled with self-identity
in seeking to answer the following questions:

- Why am I here?
- Who am I?
- What meaning is there to life?
- Who cares about me?
- Why doesn't someone, anyone, love me?
- If I am a Christian, why doesn't God help me?

I know that for some of you this situation may have never existed. But
for most of us there is real need to discover our self-worth. We discuss
this issue in great depth later on in this book so that we can learn the
value of our lives through full knowledge of Christ as Lord and Savior.
If your life has not been filled with struggles for identity and a true self-
image, then give thanks for this. However, someone you know may be
struggling deeply in this area.

As I struggled with my self-image and identity, I became misdirected. Well into my adult years I sought answers to these important
questions, but never found answers. I wasn't reading the Bible, nor did
I pray much to solve these problems. I was truly frustrated and confused
concerning my mission in life. It was not until another Christian con-
fronted me that my life began to take form and the image of Christ
became clear in me. Here I was at the age of 34—filled with anxiety,

anger, depression, frustration, and bitterness, looking for a new life. Because one person shared biblical truths with me in a common-sense fashion, my life changed.

If you struggle with your identity whether you are a believer in Christ or not, please understand this—your life is of importance to God, although perhaps you don't feel like it is. In fact perhaps nothing seems right at this point in your life. But it's true! If you sense a need for change in your life, please know that *Christ is the answer!* All you need to do is trust and believe in Christ to show you the way.

As a Christian, know that Christ has claimed you as one of His own. This in itself should give you reason to rejoice and be happy. Christ has a task for you to perform in the sharing of your faith. It may well be that someone waits to hear your words of witness about how you have been refreshed and renewed through the eternal love of Jesus Christ.

For the Christian who is willing to accept the responsibility and challenge of the Christian, life has many opportunities. He or she can experience greater happiness and a reason to live and share, with Christ as his or her example. Christians need not be overcome by any problem, for they belong to Jesus. His power is limitless! Allow Christ to work for you.

Who are you? If you have committed your life to Christ, you are a child of God. Nothing can erase His love. Remember, there is nothing you will encounter that cannot be overcome through Jesus Christ. Believe it! Accept it! Apply it to your situation!

Let's concentrate for a few minutes on different types of people. You decide where you fit in and see what new insights are yours through this discovery.

Young Persons

Have you ever heard of anyone who was born an adult? Of course not! Adam and Eve are the only two who escaped the excitement and trauma of youth. Each of us had a beginning as a tiny baby.

My beginning was filled with agony and sadness for my parents. I was born two months premature. Premature babies are not uncommon now, but in 1941 this meant almost sure death. I was born one week before Pearl Harbor was bombed. The doctor told my parents, "You might as well take her home, she won't live anyway!" (Nothing like a confident doctor, is there?)

My parents said, "You were so small that we were almost afraid to touch you. We cut handkerchiefs in half for your diapers. You were so tiny that for the first three months of your life one of us slept with our hand on you all the time. We were afraid you might stop breathing." My birth was the first of life's many challenges. But then, almost my entire life has been quite an adventure. God knew the plan for my life— live and share with others!

I can recall the excitement of my early years. Moments filled with fun, thrills, and excitement and yet moments of fear and struggling. In my youth I tried very hard to please those around me. As time wore on, it became less important and my need for God seemed to diminish. I made some foolish mistakes. Perhaps my greatest mistake was avoiding the call of God. I seemed set on pleasing myself and yet ignoring the call to love the Lord with all my heart, soul, mind, and strength. At this stage of my life, I wanted friends more than I wanted to follow Christ.

Think about your youth. Did your body seem to grow quicker than your mind? We did "dumb things" that were unpleasing to the adults around us, sometimes without understanding why we did them. Many changes seem to come at once in those growing-up years, don't they? Sometimes we couldn't understand what was happening to our bodies, and we seemed to rebel at almost anything. There were countless moments when we felt extremely restless and that life was a vacuum of nothingness. Frustrations seemed forever present. We often felt awkward and gawky. Although we sought to be "good," thoughts ran through our minds that were often mischievous. Some of us even found we were tempted to do things we knew to be wrong just to "prove ourselves" to others. The young years were surely a challenge to us.

Our parents and teachers are very important to us as we begin to develop our own identity. Words and actions of adults can give us a strong foundation to build our lives upon or else they can cause us to build on shaky and unstable ground. Words of encouragement are never out of fashion or unneeded!

Parents, please be careful how you talk around your children. Careless words can destroy happy hearts. A child who feels insecure makes few contributions. Discouragement can influence his or her way of life. A parent's love and approval are always important to a child. Although you think your young person knows you love him or her, never be neglectful in expressing the words, "I love you." Even the brightest and happiest of children need this reassurance. Love is the key to a happy life.

Teachers, your efforts do not go without notice for long. You are vital not only in teaching the basics of life but in displaying encouragement and kindness. You live outside the family structure and are the person with the strongest influence next to the parents. I worked as a classroom volunteer for more than three years at the elementary level. Not only did God teach me a great deal about children in this time, but I also acquired a great respect for teachers. Thank God for Christian teachers and their efforts to instill values, as well as knowledge, in the hearts of our young people. A good Christian school teacher is a priceless worker in the Lord's field. Without giving specific examples, take my word that their love reaches far beyond the classroom. A teacher who encourages will always be remembered in the heart of a young person.

Young Adults

Frustration does not lend itself to a select group of individuals. All ages are affected by it. However, the world is an especially exciting and frustrating place when you are between the ages of eighteen and thirty.

Men and women in this age group usually feel as though "their day" has arrived. Now it is their turn to change things and step forth with enthusiasm. Now they are finally old enough to have a say and feel they can make valuable contributions in our world. This group is ready to be listened to by the world. They feel confident and sure they can make changes for the better.

For the young adult, life has seemingly just begun. There are many new avenues and byways to travel. There are things to do, places to go, people to see. Life is exciting! Many in this group have left home to make their own way. This is "their moment," and they intend to make the best of it.

Young adults often feel they want to live life to the fullest. There are days when everything goes great. Still other days, everything seems so terribly wrong, and the bird of paradise seems to have flown the coop. The moments on the mountain tops give way to days of wandering through the valleys filled with shadows. Unpredictable highs and lows often cause periods of frustration. Young people often face the realization that they're not really going to change the world after all!

A young adult's relationship to Christ becomes important at this stage in life. Those who walk with Christ have begun to realize the necessity of a right relationship with the Savior. They have learned that life with Christ takes on special meaning. When they know Christ as Lord and Savior, they need not spend needless hours searching for the meaning of life. They have already begun to acquire a certain confidence and trust. They know in whom they believe and run their race with a purpose and plan.

Those who do not know Christ often learn in this stage how great frustration can be. Depression, restlessness, and anxiety are not uncommon. There arises a feeling of "What now?" Many young adults seem to lose their sense of direction at this point. It is difficult, at best, to cope with life when one cannot find happiness in what the world has to offer. *Real happiness is found in knowing Christ.*

Young adults have a bumpy road to travel today. Perhaps more than ever we look for great things from them. We expect these young people to uncover the mysteries of science and technology and to settle the problems inherited from days gone by. Many times they can scarcely live today, let alone conquer each tomorrow.

The years as a young adult should be a time of encouraging others as we reach our "prime time" of life. Good words, lovingkindness, and a godly example are important. Press on and focus your attention on the Lord. Frustration can be turned into an opportunity to share your trust and faith.

Single Adults

For years the single adult went practically unnoticed. Today, however, we have become increasingly aware of those who are single. Some never marry, remaining single for various reasons. My generation seemed encouraged to marry. However, today the pressure has eased, and we have many more single adults.

There was a time, not long ago, that a man was supposed to have a wife and family in order to be a "good company man." As my dad reminds me, "We had a certain job, and very few people ever changed jobs." In some groups, marriage was an expected part of life. Today's single adult is accepted more readily than they were 25 years ago.

Single adults face periods of frustration just as do married adults. Many areas of a single adult's life are strikingly similar to those of non-single adults' lives. Being single does not make an individual immune to frustration.

Within the Christian community singles have not always been treated with great kindness. The sad fact is that they are often ignored. This is not always intentional, but it does happen. We should be more sensitive to them and be willing to share with them whenever possible. I expect many of them feel almost alien to our Christian society because of neglect. We must be concerned for single adults and not exclude them from being involved in God's work.

Now, single adults, take heed! You, as members of the body of Christ, have my great respect and admiration. You may have been called to do something that I cannot do—serve the Lord in a full-time profession or calling. Please consider the challenge and opportunity you have as a single to serve the Lord. Those of us who are married have a responsibility to our spouse and our children, but you have a golden opportunity to serve Him wherever He calls you. The challenge of serving as a follower of Christ may be within your own community or church. It may be that the Lord Jesus has been pulling at your heartstrings and asking you to do more there.

Think about what Christ has told you to do, and examine your response. Would you be happier accepting a special challenge? Is there something Christ has asked you to do for Him that you continually refuse to do? You might be pleasantly surprised when you consider your personal response to Christ's call and find that now is the time to step out for Christ. Life is fullest when doing the work of the Lord Jesus Christ. There is no greater happiness than realizing God's call for you personally and responding in a positive manner. Ask yourself, "Am I ready to take up my cross and follow where Christ leads me?"

I get excited when I consider the love of the Lord for all people and when I see His Spirit change our lives. Doors of challenging opportunity may be ready to open for you. Jesus will ask you to do something that you will find rewarding. The Lord never fails those He calls but brings them to a deeper understanding and knowledge of Himself. Spiritual maturity is gained when you allow your life to be a part of the work of Christ.

Separated and Divorced Adults

If you are separated or divorced from your marriage partner, then you surely know what it's like to feel frustration. It's important that you understand that God has not forgotten you. He knows your circumstances. Perhaps you feel much like a tiny bird who has fallen from its nest. You want a new beginning, but you just aren't sure where to begin. As you flit to and fro, you seek to find the right direction. Bear in mind there is only one safe direction—toward Jesus!

Jesus cares for all His own. He knows you and waits for you to respond. The Christian who has faced the pain and frustration of divorce may suffer feelings of separation and loss. It is painful for someone you have loved to no longer love you. Please be assured that Jesus Christ continues to love you, no matter what has happened in your life.

Don't allow anything to keep you from God's love. Christian and non-Christian alike are affected by the trauma that accompanies divorce, but don't run from Jesus' help. He wants to help you through this difficult time in the best possible manner for your life. Reach out for the assurance that our Lord and Savior has for you. Focus your attention on Him, and He will give you a peace in troubled time.

No one should stand in judgment of another. Our lives should be based on the love of God at all times and not on personal opinions and ideas. Step forward and experience the security that Christ the Lord offers you.

Widowed Adults

Widowed individuals have a special heartache and burden to bear. The loss of a marriage partner is a painful experience. Frustration, grief, loneliness, and separation from someone you have spent countless years with have left you feeling very much alone. Life almost seems impossible at times as you long to be with the one who has gone before you.

I am almost at a loss to express the feelings and concerns of those who are widowed. Although I have not experienced this misfortune myself, I have seen it within my own family. I know the feeling of loss runs deep; yet it is important to remember that life is not over and God has a continuing plan. The Christian man or woman who has reached the senior years has a tremendous contribution to make to the younger set. Through his or her experiences and wisdom, we, who are a bit younger, can also learn.

To the Christian widow or widower, your Christian life and attitudes in sharing your faith help lend a supportive structure to the family of God. We need older, more mature Christians to share the knowledge and wisdom found by serving God throughout the years. Please don't allow attitudes of hurt and loss to change your direction in following the Lord. Your contribution is important. The experiences you have encountered may be used as a stepping stone for others to develop and expand their faith. Maybe a part of your life has been altered for a while, but God still desires you to be a vital part of His efforts to reach others. He knows your capabilities. He knows how to speak to your heart. Please respond to God's call in your life.

Mid-lifers

I have saved this section for this part of our study for a special reason—I fit in here! I'm not really picking on you, if you are in midlife, it is just that I am fully aware of your feelings and attitudes. Frustration has slapped you in the face from time to time, but you have refused to surrender to it. Good for you!

Midlifers are the people between thirty years of age and the senior years. We have lived long enough to recall several election campaigns and some events now classified as history. The "hurry-up" days are slowly being replaced by the "I'll-get-to-it-as-soon-as-I-can" days.

We are beginning to feel what others say about growing old. Midlife is when we decide we shouldn't play softball with the church team, because one of our children will be on the same squad. Midlife is the time we look in the mirror and observe "laughter lines" between the corner of our eyes and our hairline. Midlife is when we determine the things that are really important in our lives. For many of us the reality must be faced that our careers are at a standstill. Others of us have finally reached our career's peak, and this has caused us to consider our future.

For the man who has entered the middle years, there may be an identity struggle with questions like, "Who am I?" Television and magazines would tell us that the "macho man" is the man most women admire as he guzzles on his beer. Even worse, he is supposed to be a man who is strong and desirable, because he smokes a certain brand of cigarettes. We appear to live in a world that is confusing us just enough that we have almost forgotten what a "real man" is. If you are concerned about retaining an image of a "real man" allow me to describe the man who gains my loving respect any day. See if my standards aren't close to yours.

1. A real man loves his parents. In fact, when he is with them, hugs and kisses are never "old fashioned."

2. He loves his wife as she is, not as she was or as he wishes her to be.

3. He is not afraid to let his child cry when the need is genuine.

4. He himself is not too proud or too "manly" to cry openly when someone he loves is suffering or dies.

5. He is a man who places his faith and trust in Christ.

6. He encourages his own family by sharing the Word of God with them in principle and in practical application.

7. He *knows* in whom he believes, Christ, and shares this in a quiet, orderly example with those who know him.

8. He is caring, loving, and concerned for those of the household of faith. He has learned to share the love he has discovered in Christ with all people.

9. He is not afraid to be God's man. He knows that his heavenly Father is in control of every situation.

The real "macho man" is not a superman but a godly man. His strength is in knowing the Lord Jesus Christ as his Savior and Lord. The "real man" is a man who is feeling, honest, and true to those he loves and to his God.

Think of the men whom you personally admire and respect. What qualities do you admire in their lives? Consider Christ. What made Him different in His humanity from the man, for instance, who seeks to impress others'? When we truly consider the admirable qualities of a man, surely the "macho man" looks entirely different than he is projected on television.

The woman in midlife has her share of frustrations too! Magazines, television, and society have placed her in a role-playing position also— the "perfect woman." She is supposed to be 5 foot, 10 inches tall and weigh 98 pounds. There is no gray in her hair, for all the beauty products help rid her of "unsightly gray."

What a frustration! How could I ever stretch my 5 foot, 1 inch body an extra 9 inches? God just didn't make me tall. Sorry to say I can barely reach the bottom shelves of the cupboard, let alone look "appealing." As for the 98 pounds, well I reached that weight long ago (perhaps in my very early teens). My mother, who was built exactly like I am, once said, "You know all my family was built like us, short and stocky." It was true to my knowledge, for both of her sisters looked like us. Frankly, I don't think God intended for all of us to look exquisite and prim. God merely asks that we trust and believe that He knew us before we even existed.

For years I was frustrated about this image of woman. I really had no control over my height. The struggle to see over the crowd at a parade was almost more than I could deal with. After many years, I learned that my inward appearance was more important than my outward image. Whether short or tall, what I feel within my soul is the controlling factor of my life. If someone cannot accept me because of my physical status, then their spiritual insight is shortsighted. God made us as we are with a purpose. In fact the frustrations I have endured because I am short seldom bother me now. It's fun to look up at people, because in some instances it's the only way I will ever have the opportunity to "look up" to them.

In my estimation, the following characteristics describe what the actual midlife woman is:

1. A woman who has found an understanding of herself through the knowledge of Christ.
2. A woman who is a little less than perfect but still beautiful in the eyes of those who know her heart.

3. A woman with a bit of gray in her hair and a twinkle in her eye.
4. A woman who is still challenged by life.
5. Her children, if God has so blessed her, may be almost grown or are adults. She has done her best and made a quiet contribution to their lives. She knows the time is near when she must gently push the children from the nest.
6. She is a woman who, as a Christian, has learned the value of trusting God.
7. She is a bit restless and perhaps ready to reach forth and receive a "new challenge" from God for her life. At this moment in her life, she is ready to strive toward new goals by serving others through her strength in the Lord Jesus.
8. The midlife woman sets goals. She understands that there are many new trails to blaze as she allows Christ to work in her life.
9. She is a woman who still supports her husband and loves him. The fact is, she loves him more today than ever! She knows who the real love is in her life.

As you see from my evaluation of the woman in midlife, there is a need for involvement. I am sick of people telling me that life is over at forty. Phooey! Let go of that idea! We may shift gears at forty plus, but it's only to reach our goals without tiring too quickly. Christian woman, listen to this—you are surrounded by some of the greatest opportunities you will ever face. For many of us, our time is not filled by family and home, thus offering us the opportunity to serve the Lord in a different manner.

It's okay to slow down at forty, but for heaven's sake, don't stop and park your life at the curb! There is a challenge before you that should renew your spirit and excite your soul. Women, take heed! The Lord is calling many of us out to work in His name, and we are refusing to listen! We've parked our lives at the curb and have thrown away the keys. Many of us have given our life to the "soaps" instead of to Christ. Friend, you don't know what frustration is until you have continually denied the call of Christ. If your life is stale and meaningless, ask yourself, "What is my attitude toward Christ the Lord? Do I seek His guidance in finding happiness and purpose for my life?"

When I hear a woman in midlife say she has nothing to do, I have a great desire to share with her what God has done in my life. I used to think the same way! When I was thirty-nine years old, a friend said to me, "Did you know you can write?" Frankly, I did not! It was a passing interest but one I had never pursued. When I tried to laugh it off, my friend replied, "I'm serious!" I was surprised to see that she was serious, very serious indeed. Her words stirred my mind and challenged my heart, "You really do need to take a writing course and share your ideas."

When I asked her what she thought I should write about, she smiled and replied, "Well, I don't know, but I'm sure it would be good whatever it is!" Do you see how God supplied just the right person to give me His challenge for my life? There were only three people I knew whose judgment and ideas would have encouraged me to take up this challenge, and this woman was one of the three.

On the same evening as my conversation with this woman, Sandy, my husband, and I were chatting. I said, "I heard the funniest thing today. Let me tell you about it." I told him what my friend had said, but he didn't laugh. It puzzled me. His reply was, "I support that idea 100 percent! I feel you should enroll in a writing course of some sort. In fact, if you don't enroll on your own, I'll do it for you!" I knew Sandy was serious. He was also one of the three people whose opinions I most trusted. God can move in strange ways to convict our hearts. More often than not He uses people we know and respect to show us the truth. Sometimes it pricks deep into our spirit.

I expect there aren't too many people who take courses from the Christian Writer's Guild and submit less than six written assignments! I was so shy I didn't want to share my thoughts and ideas. After all, it had been twenty years since I graduated from Whitehaven High School in Memphis, Tennessee. I had no college education. "What did I have to offer anyone?" I asked myself. I was very insecure about the entire course, but I enjoyed writing.

I completed the course in January 1982. Then I said, "Okay God, if you want me to write, You're going to have to do something about it." He did! A gnawing feeling began to eat away at me, and I was only freed from it as I began to write. In February I submitted materials to *Love Letters* and the *Arkansas Baptist.* Both accepted my materials. (Guess who was the most surprised? Me!) When I told my friend, her reply was, "I knew you could do it! Keep on!"

Much like any writer, one little nibble at my material really nabbed me. I began to send other articles out for review and rejection. The rejection slips poured in, and I became frustrated. I prayed, "Lord, You know I can't handle this. If You want me to share my writings, show me where and how." God knows me so well. He is fully aware of the promise and commitment I made that day. I promised I would share whatever He wanted in a practical and personal manner if this was what He desired. My spirit was tossed about, knowing that something was coming of major importance and yet not knowing what to write.

From Union Gospel Press came my first major writing assignment. I received a contract to write thirteen stories for them. I was thrilled and almost giddy about the opportunity. I began to understand God's plan for me. Here I was, forty years old and challenged with a new opportunity to serve Christ. It was exciting and fun. To make my point, let me illustrate what happened to me in a short while.

- Several articles appeared in *Love Letters.*
- I was a featured writer for the column Woman's Viewpoint in the *Arkansas Baptist* in March 1983.
- Thirteen articles for Union Gospel Press.
- An assignment for a book on divorce.
- Nine more articles for Union Gospel Press.
- The first book: *A Book of Devotions for Today's Woman.*
- The second book: *Temptation: How Christians Can Deal with It.*
- The third book: *The Christian's Diary: A Personal Journal for Bible Study, Prayer, and Spiritual Growth.*
- The fourth book: *Frustration: How Christians Can Deal with It.*

All this within one year. Don't tell me there is little we can contribute at midlife! So get busy doing it! For the vast majority of those in midlife, the time to move for Christ is *now.* Do it *today!*

Senior Citizens

I believe some of the most misunderstood people in the world are our senior adults. Someone coined the term "senior citizens" to give this group a special designation. The truth is that many of our older adults aren't ready to be put on the shelf. Many of them have a great deal of enthusiasm and zest for life. Most of them are still living fairly active lives and making valuable contributions to society.

My parents often said, "Just because you're old enough to retire doesn't mean you can't be useful." I think this sums up the feelings of many older adults. They are very useful and needed in our world. Life without their wisdom would be empty.

There is a storehouse of experience and information contained within each individual's life. Those of us who are a bit younger can profit greatly from them. One thing that Christ has taught me is the value of sharing information and experiences with others. We often consider our misfortunes and problems as unique, while among us there may be people who have encountered the same hardships. It is in sharing ourselves that we grow in love toward others. We need to share our views openly and honestly.

I have a special older friend, Frankie Edwards, whom I love very dearly. For the last three years we have worked in Bible school in the same department. Frankie tells me, "I want to serve Christ as long as I can." The children quickly learn to love her and respond to her as she shares her faith in Jesus Christ. People who know Frankie have been blessed by touching lives with her. Frankie's love, patience, kindness, gentleness, and commitment to Christ illustrate a living example of His Spirit living within the heart of a child of God. I count it a joy to be a tiny part of Frankie's life. I am thankful that God has allowed us a special relationship.

We have so much to share with one another as Christians. We should be glad to talk and guide one another along the paths of life. Were it not for the guidance of our older Christians, like Frankie, many of us would have never come to know Christ as Lord and Savior.

Older adults, never feel as though your time of sharing of Christ is over. It is not! Even if you become hindered physically, there is still something you can do for Christ—you can pray. Prayer is a building block of our faith. Prayers uttered in the quietness of your heart may change many difficult situations. Exercise your faith and allow it to continue to grow with each passing day.

We have covered, ever so briefly, some of the stages of life we encounter. In each stage there is a certain element that makes life special—it is Jesus Christ. We need to comprehend the importance of gaining new insights and growing in our faith. Did you notice that within the various stages of life there is often an overlapping of experiences? Because we all are at different stages, we must remember that Christians are to support and love one another from the heart. Love is the key to life, and Christ is the doorway to understanding.

Our lives are not set by the worldly standards but by God's. We are made in His image. We are not to conform to the standards of today's world but strive to be godly individuals. Those who are unbelievers find this difficult, if not impossible, to comprehend. They seek to stretch and squeeze our Chistian beliefs and faith and conform us to their way of thinking. But recall the words of Paul in Romans 12:1, 2. "I urge you therefore, brethren, by the mercies of God, to present your bodies a living and holy sacrifice, acceptable to God, which is your spiritual service of worship. And do not be conformed to this world, but be transformed by the renewing of your mind, that you may prove what the will of God is, that which is good and acceptable and perfect." (NAS).

So then, my Christian friend, take heart! Be encouraged when you do not follow the trail leading to darkness but walk in the light with the Savior. Frustrations may come, but Christ will set us free as we focus our minds and hearts on Him. Let us move forward in our search for further understanding in dealing with frustration in our lives and the lives of others. Let your image reflect the love of Christ that you hold securely in your heart.

QUESTIONS

1. Write a brief description of the view you hold of yourself.

2. If you were to tell someone your task as a Christian, how would you describe it?

3. Why do you think we struggle with our self-image?

4. How would you describe the importance of the Christ-led life?

5. What do you think is the greatest struggle of young people in our world today?

6. What frustrations are common between the ages of eighteen and thirty?

7. Make a list of some of the challenges a person might encounter at midlife.

8. What should be our relationship to Christ, as believers, in the later years of our life here on earth?

9. Locate two Scriptures that relate to the Christian walk. Write them in your notebook.

10. What is the greatest contribution you have made thus far to the sharing of your faith and love in Christ?

11. What age group do you feel is most affected by frustration?

12. What are the strong points of the godly man?

13. Think of a woman whom you admire and respect. Does she display an awareness of Christ in her life? What makes her different from other women you have known?

14. Make a list of six things you would like others to see in your life as you journey the road of life. Be honest!

15. What keeps you from gaining the qualities listed in question 14?

16. Are you willing to pray for changes in your life that you might learn how to be victorious over frustration?

chapter
3

a variety of frustrations

> *If we spend sixteen hours a day*
> *dealing with tangible things and*
> *only five minutes a day dealing*
> *with God, is it any wonder that*
> *tangible things are 200 times more*
> *real to us than God?*
>
> William R. Inge

This chapter deals with a variety of factors leading to frustration. While trying to draw a list that is extensive, informative, and important, it is impossible to include all the reasons humans become frustrated. Simply stated, we could fill volumes with information on sources of frustration, since it is a subject that is both fascinating and alarming. Frustration deals with our emotional as well as our spiritual well-being. This chapter seeks to give the reader an in-depth understanding of the part frustration plays in lives.

Self-expectations

Who is the person who expects the most from you? More than likely it is yourself. We often find it difficult to please ourselves in even the smallest of ventures. We become unable to reach goals and maintain a reasonable standard of living, for we force ourselves into some situations that are impossible to deal with on our own.

To achieve anything within a reasonable amount of time is wonderful, but to force ourselves into situations that are impractical is foolish. Our desires are to be more, to have more, and to do more. We see people who are driven to perform tasks that others have been unable to achieve. We seek to be more than the ones who have gone before us. We are driven to excellence in the name of "meeting the challenge."

More likely than not, you have been in a situation similar to this, having decided to step forward, only to meet the uncertainty of disappointment and sometimes experience difficulties. We decide we want something, it is meant for us, and we push ourselves to great lengths to have it. In fact, we often place the desires of our hearts ahead of God. We step forth on our own, without the slightest consideration of God's plan for us. We expect to be victorious, because "we want it!" No wonder disappointment is so common in our lives! We are only happy for the moment. When we do achieve success, we commit ourselves to even more difficult tasks.

As believers, we need to be sensitive to God's plan for us. We are called upon by His Spirit to perform certain tasks of importance. When we do not listen for God's instruction, it will elude us. We need a desire to hear God speak to our souls. Only as we strive to please God can we ever please ourselves. We find happiness and purpose for life through serving Him.

The loving Christian heart will find it difficult to function within worldly standards that teach, "Do your own thing." We should know by now that "our own thing" is usually the *wrong* thing! Standards focus on pleasures and not on the love of Christ.

For over ten years there was no happiness or peace in my life. Contentment was beyond my grasp. Try as I might, I always came up short of my own self-expectations and desires. I expect most of you understand when I say, "I simply could not be pleased with anything and be happy." It seemed there was more to life, but what? I wanted more, but yet I didn't know what. What I needed was Christ.

It was not until the truth of the Scripture text from 1 Thessalonians 4:1 sank into my troubled heart that I began to comprehend God's plan for me. "Finally then, brethren, we request and exhort you in the Lord Jesus, that, as you received from us instruction as to how you ought to walk and please God (just as you actually do walk), that you may excel still more" (NAS). Although my spirit was seeking to please God, my mind was set on self-pleasure. I was the all-important one, but only to myself!

Do you see the importance of this passage? I can still excel in my efforts and goals but only through Christ. Christ is vital to my walk as a Christian, for it is through Him that I keep from stumbling over my own self-will. He renews my spirit and makes me complete in every way. My spirit can be positive, happy, fulfilled, and excited as I allow Christ to be a working part of my relationship with Him and others. I can receive victory and achieve goals because of His involvement in my life. I need not fall flat on my face. My expectations and goals had often been unrealistic. I needed to understand that I was a better person because the Holy Spirit is a part of me. I will not, I cannot, be overcome for any prolonged period of time as I walk to please God. The victories come one by one. They delight my mind and lift my spirits.

Self-expectations need not lead to bitter disappointments. Walking with Christ gives a refreshing meaning to life. He allows my spirit to rejoice and soar, because I desire to please Him. It is in Christ that each Christian finds fulfillment and reward. Christ is the key to happiness.

Lack of Direction

Who among us has not been troubled by problems that cause us to lose our sense of direction? While searching for direction we seem to come up blank. We may find an overwhelming desire to learn which steps to take, and yet we do not know what course to pursue.

Frustration can set in. This leads to confusion. We are tossed about as though we were riding the "roller coaster of life." Even as we pray, uncertainty sets in. Perhaps, we think, God has placed us on "hold." Perhaps we just have not obtained a clear connection and cannot hear what God is saying because of the noise around us. This only adds to our frustration. We feel as though we might never find a clear-cut path to follow. We are frustrated!

When lack of direction is a problem, we must learn to trust Christ totally for all of our life's needs. It may be that this is a period of testing and trying for you. Turn to James 1:2–5: "You must consider it the purest joy, my brothers, when you are involved in various trials, for you surely know that what is genuine in your faith produces the patient mind that endures; but you must let your endurance come to its perfect product, so that you may be fully developed and perfectly equipped, without any defects. But if any one of you is deficient in wisdom, let him ask God who generously gives to everyone and never reproaches one with its lack, and it will be given to him" (Williams).

You see, a lack of understanding about direction can be a positive adventure in which one can grow in godly wisdom. God does not always say, "Yes," or "No." Sometimes He very quietly and lovingly whispers, "Maybe, just maybe." God wants us to use our minds for positive thinking and generation of ideas and plans, which will allow others to see Him at work in our lives.

I recall one occasion when we couldn't decide what to do. It affected our family, my husband's job, our security, and surely tested our faith and trust in Christ as Lord of our lives. Although we prayed and prayed about what choice to make, we saw no clear answer. Instead of growing short-tempered and ill at ease, we seemed to grow in patience and understanding. We knew the answer was before us. We felt we simply had failed to recognize it. Finally, we had come to the deadline. A decision had to be made—change jobs or continue on as things were.

Sandy talked with our minister about our problem. While he visited the minister, I continued to pray at home. When Sandy returned home, I believed there would be a sure answer, some great insight from God. What our minister said did make a difference, but we still had to make a decision.

You know that our Lord Jesus Christ expects us to think and act on our own while under His loving protection. The minister had said, "Sometimes there is no clear-cut yes or no but a definite maybe. Perhaps you are being told that whatever decision you make is all right with the Lord. Just ask that He close the wrong doors and open the right ones. Believe that your decision might be guided by His loving Spirit."

Sometimes it is so simple. The fact is that we often cannot see in which direction to travel, because we are unwilling to chance it. When we understand a definite answer is not always available, we must learn to apply faith. Sandy did change jobs and began a new career as a health physics consultant. It isn't always easy. Then again, it's not supposed to be. It has been good for us, and God has blessed our lives with countless opportunities to serve Him. Sandy likes people and is an easygoing fellow. The Lord uses this and allows him the opportunity to share his faith as he travels all over the United States. Many of God's blessings are ours when we accept the uncertainties of life and allow our faith to function at total capacity.

Change of Moods

What person doesn't suffer with mood changes? Our moods may be happy one day and depressed and frustrated the next. God made men and women emotional beings. Our emotions can be a blessing or a curse, depending on how we deal with them. How often have you felt on top of the world one moment, only to feel down in the pits the next?

It is my blessing (or misfortune, sometimes I wonder) to come from a family of moody people. The people on both sides of the family seemed to be very sensitive people. My mother often referred to our family as "high strung." Indeed we were all that and a little more. Our Irish and Scot-Irish temperaments tended to rise every now and then. The results were hot tempers!

Unless I know a person well, there is within my emotional makeup a quiet nature. It is very difficult for me to talk with people I do not know or have not met. Strangers make me ill at ease. Basically, I am just not a very open person. In addition to my normally quiet manner, there is a quick temper that lends a flare of unpredictability. For years my temper would really fly at the slightest thing. Thankfully, Jesus has quieted much of it and taught me some lessons on temperament.

Now I have a tendency to sit on my temper and quench my anger, until boom! It all blows at once. There are some people who tell me, "I can't imagine you ever getting angry." If only they knew me. God got hold of my temper and taught me some important lessons about anger and restraint.

I still struggle with mood changes. Perhaps it has to do with my emotions and being very sensitive. I still tend to fall into the "mood trap." Whatever the reason, moods and feelings are my worst enemy. As I experience a change in moods, there are many foreign feelings and attitudes that enter my mind. Very often my greatest struggle is the feeling that nobody loves me. Then I feel down and really frustrated, and I develop the attitude that nobody really cares.

Changing moods can be an enemy or a friend. We can allow moments of frustration to be turned to our good, or we can allow them to set us aside on the bench and make us wait. As we sit on the bench of frustration, we become onlookers in life. We must free ourselves from this feeling and allow ourselves to be a part of the action. At such moments, we can come off the bench and become a participant in life again.

Isolation

Feelings of isolation can occur at any time. They can be the result of an illness, separation from those we love, age, or ever so many other things. Isolation is loneliness!

Have you ever been so alone that you wondered if anyone knew you were alive? Have you wondered why nobody seemed to care for you? There isn't so much as a card in the mail or a phone call. Have you become so frustrated wondering why your life must be this way? You feel as though you may be the only person left in the world that has feelings. Frustration does that to you; it makes you wonder about life.

Separation from others is loneliness at its height. We need one another. Each of us needs love and encouragement as we encounter life on a daily basis. We all have a need to be loved by someone, anyone, every day of our lives. The heart that is isolated and lonely often battles with monotony and emptiness. There seems to be no end in sight to each day, and tomorrow seems to be no different.

Many who are isolated from the mainstream of life have an illness. Perhaps there is something that keeps them from being strong and healthy. Perhaps it is age. Whatever the reason, the need is great and frustration can come quickly and linger long.

The last few years of my mother's life were challenging years for her. She could no longer see well enough to go shopping. Crowds made her nervous, and she tired quickly. She seldom left the house at all. After an operation on her left eye, things even seemed to grow worse. She said, "I just can't see well enough to get out or do anything."

Her right eye had been damaged at the age of eight, so she had struggled with the desire to see better most her life.

Mother's vanishing eyesight limited her television watching. The "soaps" which she had been so dedicated to watching for years were replaced by listening. She could scarcely read the paper at all, even with the use of a large magnifying glass. It often frustrated her as she adjusted her glasses in hope of seeing a bit better. Still mother seemed to cope.

Once we gave mother some cassette tapes on the New Testament. (Thank God for that little blessing in her life.) She said, "I take my large-print Bible and try to read along with it. I have really enjoyed those tapes." Although Mother was partially isolated from life, her faith and knowledge of Christ continued to grow. I often remember how Mother listened to those tapes and how God taught her through them. She had struggles with frustration, but she never gave up wanting to know more about Christ Jesus and grow in her understanding of Him.

Isolation need not be a bitter enemy of those who encounter various struggles. As Christians, we can take advantage of modern technology to share with other members of the household of faith who are in need. Tapes, videotaped programs, records, home Bible studies—there is so much we can do. All we need to do is decide to do it. Surely there are some among us who can touch lives and lift the spirits of others.

Too Little Involvement

I can scarcely believe there were times I was not involved enough in life, but there were. My world was nothing but one of sameness and emptiness. There was nothing to do and a lot of time to kill.

Frustration can be overwhelming when this occurs. You feel life has no purpose at all. You ask, "Why must life be like this? What am I living for? How long will it go on?" The questions reel and turn in your head, and the answers disturb your heart, "I don't know!"

I wish that during this time of my life, which lasted several years, someone would have come to me and set me straight. Life need not be filled with this sort of frustration at all. Most of these feelings are brought on by a lack of involvement in anything at all. Had I known what I know now, perhaps things would have been different. Nobody ever told me about volunteer programs. I suppose there weren't that many programs available, but still there are many opportunities to reach out to help others if we only look.

Had someone told me about the need for volunteers in the public school system, I surely would have responded. Had I been involved in a church that was ministering to the needs of others, there would have been something I could have done. I was growing stale.

Here I was, a married woman, sitting around doing nothing from age twenty-one to twenty-nine. During this time I didn't receive one call from the churches we attended, a visit, a card, anything. Yet we produced nothing either. It would have been a glorious opportunity for someone to step forward and share their love and faith, but no one did. Maybe that is why those years were so difficult for me. Nothing, absolutely nothing, spiritual happened. I struggled. I didn't know the Bible, nor did I seek to understand it because I thought, "It's too difficult for me. I'm not intelligent enough to understand it."

So many wasted years—the "good-time years"—during which little was accomplished. Oh, how miserable I felt inside!

Nothing to do? Sure there is something to do! If you are at this point, get busy! Get involved in something productive. Stop dwelling on yourself, and don't give frustration and resentment the upper hand. Volunteer for library work; be a school volunteer; help at church; visit the aged, the young, the sick; make phone calls for the church; start a Bible study (even if you don't know how). Become involved in life. Live for Christ today! Place your eyes on Christ. Commit your heart to Him. Allow yourself the freedom to give away a little of yourself. Watch the joy grow in your life.

Too Much Involvement

When do you say "no"? How do you know there is too much going on in your life at one time? Too much involvement is almost as bad as too little involvement.

It is not difficult to become overloaded. A willing worker for any cause faces this danger. Nothing is more frustrating than spreading yourself too thin. When you really get involved in living for Christ, watch out for danger signals. There are too few willing to do the work of many. There is a need to maintain a happy balance in any project you are involved in, especially in the family of God.

It isn't easy to say, "I just can't do any more." We want to do more, and we see the need to be about the important tasks at hand, but still there is a limit to our involvement. When we become loaded down in our efforts, we can become bogged down. We quickly encounter frustration. Nothing seems to get done the right way, because we can't decide what to do. There is a necessity for us to understand that we need only do a few things well and not a lot of things half way.

Even if a program must suffer because of your lack of involvement, sometimes it must be so. God wants you to be sure about your areas of involvement whether in the church, community, job, or home. There should be prayer for guidance. Ask God to show you the things that are important to Him. Choose wisely. You may not have understood that Satan can whisper in your ear and tell you that you are the only one to carry out a certain task. Satan doesn't mind you getting a full load by doing the work of the Lord. In fact, the more involved you are the less likely you are to function properly. Too much involvement renders a Christian ineffective.

Consider the half-done job and its worth. There could be someone who wants the chance to take on one of the tasks you have as a burden. Surely there should be a limit on the areas of your activities. Some of us can handle more than others, but none can handle the bulk of the load alone. There must be a careful examination, and a regular one, about our areas of involvement. Remember to keep enough time to enjoy your family, to enjoy fellowship with other Christians, and to learn and develop new spiritual insights. The Christian who is too involved is often too busy to learn from the Word of God. Always allow time for fellowship and prayer with the Father in your schedule. You also need some free time to rest and relax.

Anxiety, Anger, and Worry

We consider the importance of these three elements in the next two chapters. Since they are of such importance to our understanding of frustration, we will consider them in depth. True knowledge and understanding of these elements are vital in overcoming what frustration seeks to do to our spiritual nature.

Communication

Is there anything more frustrating than trying to communicate with a person who will not listen? Perhaps the person will not allow you to state your view. Maybe the person rudely interrupts you time and time again in an effort to make a point or carry the bulk of the conversation.

My husband tells me that, in the business world, it is most frustrating to make a presentation to a client and have him or her mentally click off the "listen switch." After my husband spends a great amount of time and effort to form a presentation, the client doesn't listen. It may be that he or she does not think the information is important. Possibly the client feels the service is not needed, or else he or she just isn't interested. For the working person, this can be very frustrating indeed!

Still another problem with communication can be seen in marriage. Oftentimes one partner or the other is preoccupied with other thoughts. The husband's mind is still at the office. He may be worrying about a report he is involved in. The wife may have waited all day for a chance to share her thoughts with him, only to notice that she is talking to herself. Proper communication in the marriage relationship is very important. It takes effort on the part of both partners to keep the lines of communication and listening open.

Crime

We are witnesses to a growing crime wave that seems to be making the entire world its victim. Crimes that were almost unknown in years past are now commonplace. It seems as though crime is running rampant with little restriction placed on the wrongdoer.

Even gang raping has become common. People have been known to stand about, watching, as others defile the body of another. "Do whatever feels good" seems to be the attitude of the day. Murder is all about us. Senseless murders, beatings, the strong taking advantage of the weak, shoplifting, shootings, the list seems almost endless. No wonder we become frustrated about the crime problem.

We often wonder, "Is there nothing that can be done?" Why do we willingly stand by and watch someone wronged? Are we not willing to take a stand for what we know to be right? We have become a people who turn away from having a genuine concern for others. Too often we resist helping when we know that our involvement can make a difference. We almost seem fearful of doing what we know we must in order to follow the commandments of God.

Jesus said, "This is My commandment, that you love one another, just as I have loved you. Greater love has no one than this, that one lay down his life for his friends. You are My friends, if you do what I command you" (John 15:12–14 NAS). Clearly we are taught the importance of loving one another. It is in loving that we display our greatest concern for others.

Another key verse to consider about the state of the world and spiritual warfare is found in 1 John 3:9–11: "No one who is born of God practices sin, because His seed abides in him; and he cannot sin, because he is born of God. By this the children of God and the children of the devil are obvious: anyone who does not practice righteousness is not of God, nor the one who does not love his brother. For this is the message which you have heard from the beginning, that we should love one another" (NAS).

Our carnal world has sought to move itself away from God's love. It seems the time is right for the Christian community to take a stand on what is right and wrong. Until we take a stand, there will be no true change in our society. We can make the difference, but we must become involved. It isn't just a cute cliché to say, "Love one another from the heart." It is a command from God. "Be devoted to one another in brotherly love; give preference to one another in honor; not lagging behind in diligence, fervent in spirit, serving the Lord; rejoicing in hope, persevering in tribulation, devoted to prayer, contributing to the needs of the saints, practicing hospitality. Bless those who persecute you; bless and curse not. Rejoice with those who rejoice, and weep with those who weep" (Romans 12:10–15 NAS).

Worldly values that seem to slip a little deeper into the mud with each passing day will not change until Christians begin to do something. God has given us standards and rules to follow. What will happen if we don't take action and shed the light of Christ into these dark areas of life? How will the futures of our children, grandchildren, and future generations be affected? Frustrations will only deepen as acts of violence grow more commonplace. Frustration, when fully grown, displays the dark side of the personality, the result of which is great unhappiness and misery.

Additional Frustrations

It is time to gain a foothold on attitudes that tend to frustrate us. Following is a list of more things that can cause frustrations to creep into our minds. This is a perfect opportunity for you to make your own personal evalution of frustration. Why not take notes? Write your thoughts in a special notebook as you study this subject. Here are some additional ideas I had on areas of frustration:

- *Bitterness:* Bitterness toward someone or perhaps about an event that occurred in your life can pull you apart inside and out. It will encourage the seed of resentment to grow in your heart. Bitterness can change your entire attitude if it is not kept in check.

- *Pressure:* There are countless pressures that tend to weigh us down. We are never isolated from pressure. Very often the more we "stew" over a situation the worse it tends to get. Perhaps the pressures have something to do with our job. It may even be a person we work with each day who causes us great pressure. There may be someone who likes to pick at us, hurting our feelings. Possibly our pressure is due to something very personal. There are many personal pressures placed on us within our home and community. Another pressure point occurs when something or someone causes a threat to your security, thus also allowing frustration to gain a foothold in your life.

- *Grievance:* Grief is a sad experience. It is also a frustrating one. More often than not it causes extreme loneliness. In our hearts there is a mixture of sorrow and separation. After the loss of a loved one it takes time to adjust to life without his or her presence. How frustrating it is wanting to share something with the one who has left you! "Just once more. If only I could tell him or her." It's so very hard! I know, for I've been there too.

  Grief from separation or loss of a partner through divorce can also cause great frustration. It isn't easy to give up someone you have loved, no matter what the reason for the divorce. It hurts! Frustrated, defeated, bewildered at a sense of loss, often wondering what will happen next, the victims of divorce encounter definite frustration in their efforts to pick up their lives and go on.

  Another source of frustration caused by grief comes from losing one's possessions by some unfortunate act of nature. Floods, fires, tornados, and hurricanes come, and many precious belongings are lost. Frustration is a common feeling in these times. "What can I do but begin again?" we ask.

- *Restless nature:* I was born with a restless nature. I cannot seem to sit for long periods of time. There always seems to be plenty to do. My idea of resting is moving furniture. I also enjoy working with my hands. A person who has a feeling of restlessness can easily be frustrated.

  I admit that since I made a full commitment of my time to Christ I am not nearly as restless. Restlessness is the result of various needs and desires within us. For some there is a need to change jobs. For others the move to a new place will ease this restlessness. Frustration and uneasiness may be common when this type of person stays in one place for a prolonged period of time.

  Restlessness can be caused by something you feel you want to do. Perhaps your heart says, "Take a long vacation. Have a good time!" While this may not be possible, the desire is still strong. Frequently our feelings and attitudes are the basis for decision making. Without the loving guidance of our Lord Jesus Christ, it is difficult to maintain a proper balance in our lives and control our frustration. We all need Christ.

- *Great expectations and bitter disappointments:* We could spend hours discussing this problem. When we have set our goals, developed our ideas, worked on a project, and then have come up with something other than planned, the enemy of disappointment enters in. We become easily frustrated at our failures. Yet we rejoice very little over the victories which come our way. The truth is our expectations are difficult to achieve. When we fail, frustration pounds us into the sidewalks of life. We are beaten down and bruised because we have not fully achieved our goal. This attitude can be difficult to overcome and can cause many heartaches.

- *Money:* If you haven't been frustrated in this area of your life, then I am most happy for you. Money is a very real part of gaining the things we need to live. Some need money only for the necessities of life. For others it is a force that carries them to extremes. Money or the lack of it can cause a great many frustrations.

- *Uncertainties of life:* As we struggle with the things we cannot handle, we tire quickly. Often things happen that we must just accept and go on with life. Those who cannot conform to these conditions are torn by frustration. We must let Christ lead us and teach us how to respond to these unpredictable happenings, so that we can learn to cope. We can, within ourselves, do very little to change many things that occur in our lives. It is for this reason that the Christian must know who is in charge of his or her life. While we do the best we can, uncertainties do present problems. Nevertheless, as we place our faith on the front lines of life and allow it to function for us, we will receive strength from the Master.

As you see, our list can go on and on. But we must move on to explore the attitudes toward frustration in our lives.

Attitudes toward Frustration

Some people belong to the "this-too-shall-pass" club. It seems they do nothing to overcome frustration for they feel that in time it too will go away. They leave it alone; they ignore the fact that frustration is pulling at their heart. "It's only a passing thing," they say.

While it is true that frustration will eventually pass, still those nagging feelings persist. Much like an upset stomach, frustration doesn't get much better unless something is done to ease it. The method of curing frustration varies from person to person.

Frustration is a twofold problem combining spiritual and mental confusion.

The "how-did-this-ever-happen-to-me?" person has a most difficult time with frustration. First and foremost, we must remember that frustration is a common occurrence. Remember, we have called it the *frustration flu.* We need to treat it as such. It is in our reacting to life's struggles that we either go forward or slip backward. Frustration can be either a friend or an enemy. It depends on how we relate to it. God wants us to grow through the moments of frustration and trial that we encounter. He wants us to step forward, knowing that through these experiences we become wiser and more understanding of Christ's love for us.

Frustration can be turned to work for our good with very little effort. We need only look at the situation and understand there is something positive in it. Perhaps it is even time to reevaluate our priorities in life. What is important to us? Where are our thoughts focused? Who is leading our life? What is it that is so difficult to understand in this hour of frustration? And, lastly, are we truly sensitive to the Holy Spirit and His presence in our life?

The Christian need not look at these various times of frustration as setbacks. We should consider them as opportunities to grow and mature in faith. It is for our benefit that these things come to us.

Times of frustration are opportunities to discover our strengths as well as our weaknesses. It is a time for learning to give thanks, yes, in "all things," for Christ is at work in our life. Through Christ these situations can be turned into positive lessons from the One who loves us the most. Let us allow Christ the opportunity to work with us as we study. Let us receive encouragement in the knowledge that is yet to be revealed.

There is no need to allow these moments to overpower us. Recall the words of the Scriptures, "My God will amply supply your every need, through Christ Jesus, from His riches in glory" (Philippians 4:19 Williams). Your timing and God's timing may not be the same. He will give you the things you truly need. He will allow you to rejoice in knowing that He has your needs on the top of His "master list." When the Lord is ready for you to accomplish a certain task, be assured that nothing will hinder your goal from becoming a reality.

QUESTIONS
1. Why do our self-expectations cause problems in our lives?

2. How does God view us when we succeed?

3. How does He view us when we fail?

4. Look at 1 Thessalonians 4:1. What instructions are we given in the matter of our Christian walk?

5. What are the dangers of lack of direction in our lives?

6. How does a Christian find the right direction to follow in his or her life?

7. Describe the importance of trusting God for all things.

8. Locate four Scriptures that support the need to trust God.

9. Describe your moods and the manner in which they change.

10. What are some of the frustrations that are most common in your life?

11. Reread John 15:12–14. What is the importance of love according to these verses? Do you think we follow this commandment as God intended us to?

12. In Romans 12:10–15 we are given several things to do. Make a detailed list of what we are told to do. This list is good to keep tucked away for later reference. It will refresh your mind and encourage your heart.

13. What seems to be the common approach to frustration?

14. How does frustration gain control of your life from time to time?

15. What is the blessing found in Philippians 4:19?

16. What need do you want the Lord to assist you with?

17. Ask a fellow Christian to pray with you for an answer to this need. Make a bond to share your needs with someone. How can this strengthen your faith?

18. List three ways in which you are sure God has helped you this week.

chapter
4

anxiety and anger

*Anger is an acid that can do more
harm to the vessel in which it's
stored than to anything on which
it's poured.*
Baptist Beacon

The roles of anxiety and anger are significant in building areas of frustration. The combination of feelings and responses achieved by these elements can be shattering. We will first contemplate anger and its effect on our mental and spiritual well-being.

Anger is a combination of our temperament and of taking positions that express our displeasure about a given situation. In some instances these responses have built an invisible wall around us, which stands firmly rooted and hides our real selves. Responses can easily act as a shield to protect us from personal sufferings. Still other reactions can weaken our character, allowing us to become almost unapproachable people. At any rate, anger in itself is not a sin; it is how we handle it that is the deciding factor.

We must understand how anger can separate us from the love of God. It grows within, something like a spiritual tumor that can erupt at the wrong moment. Anger lashes out. We want to get even or to do justice for something that has bothered us for some time. Pressures build and must be released.

Frustration in Anger

Let's examine some examples of anger as found in the Scriptures. It is important that we realize that frustrations are often on-going experiences that, until dealt with adequately, only enlarge with time. Consider what part frustration must have played in each of these cases.

Our biblical illustrations will guide us into new areas of understanding anger. You will, of course, realize that frustration, although not called by that name, is present in each of these situations.

MOSES

Moses faced more than his share of frustration with the people of Israel. God gave Moses the task of leading the Israelites from Egypt to the "Promised Land." The journey was not without its share of problems, however, as Moses led the people through the long trip in the wilderness of the desert. Moses is quite concerned for his people and a unique problem. His feelings often result in frustration as the journey lengthens. Moses understands his need for God, but the people do not see their need.

Pharaoh had set the Israelites free after God caused a series of plagues to fall over the land of Egypt. After releasing the captives, Pharaoh decided he wanted them back. His plan was to capture the people between the Red Sea and Migdol (see Exodus 14). As the Israelites journeyed along, their anxiousness began to grow. They were afraid as they glanced back over their shoulders. They could hear the horses and chariots storming through the desert. Theirs was a very real problem. Frustration grew stronger with each passing moment. They did not want to be recaptured. What were they to do? It would be difficult to battle the Egyptians, for they were not equipped to do so. Their running room would end at the Red Sea. This was a life-and-death situation. They had forgotten their greatest weapon was God, and they feared greatly what was about to happen.

Moses told the people, "Do not fear! Stand by and see the salvation of the Lord which He will accomplish for you today; for the Egyptians whom you have seen today, you will never see them again forever" (Exodus 14:13 NAS). In this moment their eyes were taken from their godly leader, Moses; for they had almost completely forgotten about God being with them.

Moses was surely concerned that his people did not understand the power of God. He was amazed at their lack of trust in God. That day, God worked an awesome miracle through His servant Moses. I expect you know the story, but allow me to refresh your memory. As Moses stretched out his hand over the Red Sea, it parted. The sons of Israel crossed over the Red Sea without getting wet. They trekked between a wall of water on their left and a wall of water on their right. They were completely safe. When the Egyptians tried to cross over, God brought down a flood of water which drowned every rider and charioteer. With the overcoming of this problem, the people began to rejoice. They sang praises to God. This moment of frustration had been dealt with by the living God.

As we know, the Israelites were frequently frustrated during the forty-year journey. They refused to trust God for all their needs. The fact is they often overlooked the little things God provided for them. They complained frequently and loudly.

This story illustrates an important truth for our lives today. We too become frustrated. We tend to complain about every situation we encounter. We tend to overlook the blessings God has given us. We too want more. A close examination of our lives might reveal that we take from God the things we need but seldom give anything of ourselves in return.

Moses was often frustrated with the people as he sought to lead them into safety as a shepherd his sheep. But somehow they found other areas of complaint that presented danger and problems. Moses was the shepherd of a people who were often unwilling to follow. They were a restless people. They had a difficult time believing and trusting the promises of God. In the end, Moses led his flock to the "Promised Land," but he himself was not allowed to enter. Moses died, and Joshua took charge of the group.

SAMSON

If ever there was a story filled with both excitement and frustration, the story of Samson fits the requirements. His story is found in the Old Testament book of Judges. Turn with me to the fourteenth chapter. Three chapters are devoted to the telling of this magnificent story.

Samson was a strong man who had been blessed by the Lord. His strength lay in his long hair. (To gain all the details, read the story for yourself. It's an interesting and exciting story.) Samson's weakness was his desire for the harlot Delilah. The lord of the Philistines convinced her to use her powers to overcome Samson. Delilah lead Samson to believe that she loved him. He felt she could be trusted with his greatest secret—the source of his strength.

No sooner had Samson whispered his secret to her than his downfall began. As he slept on her knees, she cut off his seven locks of hair. When he awoke he learned that the power of the Lord had left him, and he was taken prisoner. He felt frustrated and angered.

He could do nothing to restore his strength. He had become a prisoner of the Philistines and was now powerless. Time and time again his thoughts must have drifted to the reason for his downfall. Samson wanted to get even with his enemies at any cost!

The Philistines had not thought that Samson's hair would grow and his strength might be restored. As the lords assembled at the temple for the sacrifice to Dagon, their god, they had Samson brought to them. They praised their god for having brought Samson to his knees. My, how they poked fun at the once strong man. They laughed at him as he stood before them. They did not realize that Samson was about to gain his revenge.

Samson, who was blinded because his captors had gouged out his eyes, had a boy station him between the pillars which served as the foundation for the temple. Samson leaned on them and called out to the Lord, " 'O Lord God, please remember me and please strengthen me just this time, O God, that I may at once be avenged of the Philistines for my two eyes.' And Samson grasped the two middle pillars on which the temple rested, and braced himself against them, the one with his right hand and the other with his left. And Samson said, 'Let me die with the Philistines!' And he bent with all his might so that the house fell on the lords and all the people who were in it. So the dead whom he killed at his death were more than those whom he killed in his life" (Judges 16:28–30 NAS).

Wow, what a story! Samson's frustration and anger were vented in a somewhat strange fashion, which resulted in many deaths. Samson had allowed his carnal desires for the woman Delilah to change his life. Notice that Samson did seek the Lord and desire to be filled with the power of God in the end. Samson's frustration and anger were an example not only to the Philistines but to those of us who live today.

HERODIAS

There is an old saying about a woman's fury. The following example of frustration and anger is found in the Gospel of Mark. Turn to chapter 6 with me and discover another type of frustration. Beginning with verse 14 we see that John the Baptist has his hands full. He has angered King Herod, Herodias (the wife of the king's brother with whom Herod is involved), and Herodias' daughter. John the Baptist had stated that the life style the king and his sister-in-law were living was wrong. Simply stated, John said it was improper to have an affair with your brother's wife.

Herodias bore a grudge against John. She wanted him put to death. She made her desire known to her daughter, who came to Herod and asked a birthday favor. Herod agreed to do whatever she desired. She in turn asked for John the Baptist's head on a platter. Do you see how the web of frustration weaves its way? Herodias had become frustrated knowing she could do nothing about John on her own. She then plans and schemes and finally gets results. Now we see King Herod is, perhaps, more than a little frustrated about this request. But having made a promise to the young girl, he must follow through on his word.

The executioner was sent out to behead John. On his return the girl was handed a platter containing the head of John the Baptist. She quickly handed it over to her mother, who was most pleased. One wonders if this did not lead to additional frustrations for both the king and the girl. Herodias' plan proved nothing other than additional frustration. No doubt there was little happiness over this incident. How could there be any happiness from taking a life needlessly?

Anger need not be nurtured and fed until it becomes sin. Anger can be set aside. Remember, anger in itself is not a sin, but it is how we deal with it that makes the difference.

JESUS

Jesus had His moments of frustration too! Let's note some of the events in Jesus' life that were frustrating. Bear in mind that Jesus never allowed anger or negative feelings to take root in Him.

A Prophet without Honor. Surely Jesus faced frustration head on many times. Remember when He went to Nazareth and the people misunderstood His teachings? Turn to the Gospel of Mark 6:1–6. Jesus taught the people some astonishing new truths. They were not ready for new insights and knowledge to be shared among them. The people were unwilling to accept Jesus' words and questioned His credentials. Imagine the frustration our Lord faced at this moment.

First the people thought of Jesus merely as the son of a carpenter. Where did He get the schooling necessary to speak as an Authority? Where did Jesus gain such wisdom and insight? Maybe they thought that God used only the most qualified and the greatest scholars to teach others. If so, they were mistaken. God uses anyone He desires to carry the message of the Gospel. Even in our time God selects those whom He wishes. It is not always those who choose to who do the work! God will and can use anyone to work for Him. Too often we seemingly limit others by their lack of education or other qualifications. We measure their abilities according to the yardstick of our own faith. We limit God by our own standards.

Second, the people questioned Jesus' background. He came from a family of carpenters ... just average people, and yet this Man was speaking as a Prophet! How can this be? They would not acknowledge Christ as a Prophet in His own time. His life did not conform to their standards. It never did! Look at what Jesus said on the subject, "A prophet is not without honor except in his home town and among his own relatives and in his own household" (Mark 6:4 NAS).

How very true are the words of Jesus. It is difficult for those who know you personally to accept you as an authority on a given subject. They know all too well your shortcomings and faults. In Jesus' case there was a problem in the eyes of the people, not with His shortcomings but with His family and background. This was an extremely frustrating situation, but Jesus shifted his focus from frustration to concern about their lack of faith and unbelief. It would have been to their credit to honor our Lord and see many miracles worked in the name of the Lord God.

In summary, many of our greatest heroes have come from humble beginnings. They share the common bond of a heritage that is rooted in life's common soil. They are gifted people with God-given abilities to perform certain tasks.

Jesus and the Storm. Jesus was tired. He had been teaching the multitude for a great deal of time. As He climbed into the boat, He said, "Let us go over to the other side" (Mark 4:35b NAS). After the boat had pushed away from shore, Jesus fell asleep. A fierce storm blew in, casting large waves over the boat. Still Jesus slept.

The men became afraid. They did not know what they should do. Possibly they had never been in such a storm before. The boat was rapidly filling with water. Finally they woke up Jesus and told Him what was happening. Jesus was bothered by their attitude. The men had thought they would surely perish in the angry sea. Jesus quieted the storm with a few words, "Hush, be still" (Mark 4:39c NAS). Then Jesus turned His attention to the disciples and said, "Why are you so timid? How is it that you have no faith?" (Mark 4:40b NAS). Did they not understand that He was the Son of God? Why did they struggle with the fear that God would allow the storm to overtake them? Jesus understood and knew that these men had many lessons to learn concerning faith. Likewise, He knows our struggles and need to grow in faith.

Anxiety

Anxiety is still another face frustration wears. It walks hand in hand with feelings that foster wrong attitudes. Anxiety is a problem that must be effectively dealt with or it will soon control much of our will power. Anxiety seeks to set us aside and make us wonder where our strength lies. Let's look at some examples of frustration resulting from anxiety.

LAZARUS' SISTERS

Lazarus, the brother of Mary and Martha, was a close and dear friend of our Lord's. His story is of great interest as we consider the role of anxiety and perhaps some anger surrounding his death.

Turn to the fourth Gospel in the New Testament—the book of John. Let's read chapter 11. Jesus knew His friend would be dead before He arrived at Bethany. By the time Martha saw Jesus come into view, Lazarus had been dead for four days. She was very anxious and distressed. Why had Jesus not come before? She ran to meet Him and said to Him, "Lord, if You had been here, my brother would not have died" (John 11:21b NAS). She knew that Jesus could make things right again if He so willed it. She trusted Jesus, but in her sorrow and grief she had become anxious for her brother to live again. She had not expected Lazarus to die.

Jesus went to the tomb where Lazarus lay buried. In an expression of grief and sorrow, Jesus wept. Everyone saw the sorrow Jesus felt. They knew His love for this man had been great. Jesus was deeply moved by the loss of His friend. Jesus prayed to His Father and asked that God use this moment to reassure the people around them. Then He spoke the words that are familiar to each of us, "Lazarus, come forth" (John 11:43b NAS).

The anxiety disappeared, and there was instant rejoicing and giving thanks to our Lord. Moments of anxiousness need not turn us away from the Lord. In fact it is best to seek out the will of the Lord in any situation. Lazarus lived—he gained new life through Christ our Lord.

JESUS AND THE DISCIPLES

John 14:1–31 records a conversation Jesus had with His disciples. He told them that He must soon go away. But He promised He would return. The disciples were anxious to know what would happen. How would they carry on without Jesus? When would He return to them? And why must it be so? They were struggling with the fact that they would lose their security and with the idea that their Leader must go away. They were anxious to know what would happen next.

Anxiety and fear of the unknown can be dangerous traps. Listen to the words of comfort Jesus spoke to the disciples. "Let not your heart be troubled; you believe in God, believe also in Me. In My Father's house are many dwelling places; if it were not so, I would have told you. I go to prepare a place for you. And if I go and prepare a place for you, I will come again and receive you to Myself; that where I am, there you may be also. And where I go you know, and the way you know" (John 14:1–4 NKJV).

Do you see that the feelings the disciples felt were well known by Jesus? Jesus was concerned for them. Jesus knew they needed the reassurance He gave to them. They were soon to realize the truthfulness of His message.

We too are to be anxious for nothing, for He has our best interests at heart. It is in understanding this that the first steps to victory are ours. Paul teaches us in Philippians 4:6 an important lesson about anxiety, "Be anxious for nothing, but in everything by prayer and supplication, with thanksgiving, let your requests be made known to God; and the peace of God, which surpasses all understanding, will guard your hearts and minds through Christ Jesus" (NKJV).

You see, God doesn't want us to be bound by the chains of anxiety and the problems that lock it in place. He wants us to travel in proper style. We should know that we have nothing to fear. Realize that in Christ we are made complete, whole, Christlike. When we understand which steps to take, anxiety need not limit our joy of being in Christ. Let us press on and gain a new understanding of "being in Christ." Let's learn to be His children in every sense of the word.

JONAH

The little book of Jonah tells a fascinating story about a man who not only was disobedient to God but also had a strange encounter. Jonah was sent by God to the city of Nineveh to preach and share the Word of God. Jonah was afraid, for the people of this city were wicked. He so feared what would happen to him if he went there that he ran away.

Jonah went to Joppa and boarded a ship. He determined in his mind that these wicked people would never get their hands on him. What Jonah had forgotten was that God's hand of justice and fairness reaches everywhere. God dealt with Jonah in a special manner, and it is recorded for all to read in the Bible. Turn with me to the book of Jonah in the Old Testament.

In Chapter 1:3–16 is the story of Jonah's efforts to elude God. As the ship sailed for Tarshish the Lord sent a great wind. The men were afraid! They did not know who or what was responsible for the anger of God which lashed against the sides of the ship. Jonah admitted to the men that it was he who was the cause of the problem and that God was angry with him.

Surely these men were frustrated beyond belief. Here they were on the sea in a killer storm about to perish, and the man who is the cause of the entire problem stands before them saying, " 'Pick me up and throw me into the sea, and it will become calm. I know that it is my fault that this great storm has come upon you.' Instead, the men did their best to row back to land. But they could not, for the sea grew even wilder than before. Then they cried to the Lord, 'O Lord, please do not let us die for taking this man's life. Do not hold us accountable for killing an innocent man, for you, O Lord, have done as you pleased.' They then took Jonah and threw him overboard, and the raging sea grew calm. At this the men greatly feared the Lord, and they offered a sacrifice to the Lord and made vows to him. But the Lord provided a great fish to swallow Jonah, and Jonah was inside the fish three days and three nights" (Jonah 1:12–17 NIV).

Inside a fish for three days! Don't you imagine that Jonah had a great deal of time to consider his disobedience to God? The more he thought about his present frustration, the more he wished he had not said no to God.

Jonah's problem resulted from his breaking faith and trust in God. He had not trusted God to take care of him and to teach him what was best for his life. He thought that God had surely made a mistake. But now, inside this smelly fish he knew that God was in control. We see from chapter 2 that Jonah dedicated himself to prayer. Jonah was reassured, through his prayer, that God would deliver him. He cried out to the Lord, and the Lord God reacted. Jonah was vomited up onto the dry land.

Now Jonah's frustrations did not end here. You see, Jonah's commitment to God was only in part. Read on in the story for additional insight about the man who wanted to serve God on his own terms. Chapter 3:1–4 says, "Now the word of the Lord came to Jonah the second time, saying, 'Arise, go to Nineveh the great city and proclaim to it the proclamation which I am going to tell you.' So Jonah arose and went to Nineveh according to the word of the Lord. Now Nineveh was an exceedingly great city, a three days' walk. Then Jonah began to go through the city one day's walk; and he cried out and said, 'Yet forty days and Nineveh will be overthrown' " (NAS). Through Jonah's efforts the people of Nineveh turned away from their wicked ways. They repented, and God did not cause their destruction. But Jonah was displeased with God's change toward the people. He became angry.

Jonah was very angry and prayed to God. Jonah, not living within God's will, prayed that his life be taken from him. He left the city and began to walk in an easterly direction. He found a place to construct a shelter and sat there. Jonah's frustration had led him to do something many of us often do—he began to concentrate on how he looked before all the world. The longer he sat there, the more the frustration grew.

God made a plant to grow over Jonah and give him shade. You see, God had not forgotten about Jonah. He was concerned for his welfare and wanted Jonah to reconsider his life. The plant produced a considerable amount of shade, and Jonah was very pleased. But Jonah still sat there dwelling on the past and wondering why God had not destroyed the people of Nineveh. Jonah had his attention focused on the wrong areas. He had decided what God should do and was sure that God had made the wrong decision. Jonah had done something that could not escape God's attention—he would not let God be God. He questioned God's authority and reasoning in dealing with these people.

God was not finished with Jonah. The next day a worm, a tiny worm, became a vital part of Jonah's plight. The worm came and ate away at the plant. The plant withered, and the sun beat down on Jonah. The wind blew against his face. Jonah questioned, "Why have you done this to me God? Why not just let me die?" Perhaps Jonah was merely lashing out at God, but God's reply to him was very special. "Then the Lord said, 'You had compassion on the plant for which you did not work, and which you did not cause to grow, which came up overnight and perished overnight. And should I not have compassion on Nineveh, the great city in which there are more than 120,000 persons who do not know the difference between their right and left hand, as well as many animals?' " (Jonah 4:10, 11 NAS).

At this point, consider the feeling Jonah must have had in his spirit. It is my belief that Jonah's frustration was dealt with at this moment. Jonah, listening to the voice of God, having examples before him, understood the importance of compassion. He had witnessed the compassion God had for him. Jonah must decide at this moment whether to set aside his own selfish attitude or to continue living a self-centered life. The decision was his.

QUESTIONS

1. How can anger influence your mind during periods of frustration?

2. Is anger a sin?

3. What are three ways to control anger?

4. Consider Moses' dilemma. How do you think Moses felt as he led the people on that long journey through the desert and the wilderness?

5. Do you think Samson's act of revenge was done in anger, frustration, or vengeance?

6. Why was Samson determined to punish so many for his downfall?

7. Do you think the feeling of frustration Herodias had for John the Baptist was justified enough to demand his head on a platter? How cruel do you consider this act of hate?

8. Do you think Jesus was frustrated with the people on His visit in Nazareth?

9. In the example of Mark 4:35, why do you think Jesus was bothered by the actions of His disciples?

10. Express the feelings you experience when you are faced with frustration.

11. How can these feelings be set aside?

12. Reread the Scripture verses found in John 14:1–31. What words of encouragement are found there?

13. How do you think the disciples were able to deal with their frustrations when Jesus said He would be leaving them?

chapter
5

worry

> *Worry is faith in the negative, trust
> in the unpleasant, assurance of
> disaster, and belief in
> defeat.... Worry is a magnet that
> attracts negative conditions; faith is
> a more powerful force that creates
> positive circumstances.... Worry is
> wasting today's time to clutter up
> tommorow's opportunities with
> yesterday's troubles.*
>
> William A. Ward

The quotation beginning our chapter is ever so true. Worry is negative action placed in our lives resulting in negative faith. Worrying produces nothing constructive. The fact is it separates us from the loving arms of the Father. It pulls us apart from His security and causes unhappiness.

The more we tend to worry, the more we are drawn from the awareness of Christ. We focus on the problem not the solution to our misery. Christians, we need to be careful about the ideas we allow to control our thought processes. True enough, there may be moments when we have strong concerns, but worry as a way of life is sinful. Worry is the result of allowing your life to shift from godly thoughts to worldly situations.

Thoughts

Daily pressures are ever present. Each day has enough problems of its own without creating more. But there are many among us who have accepted worry as a pattern of living. For these people, it isn't enough to wrestle with life's problems day in and day out, they usually create more problems to worry about. Life is filled with opportunities that either develop our spiritual insights or cause us to quench the Spirit. How we deal with daily pressures and problems is most important.

We have a free choice to say yes or no to most of our problems. We can allow pressures to build and enlarge our problem, or we can set them aside and forget them. Attitudes are ever so important! We must consider whether the positive or the negative will rule. The choice is ours, and each decision is important.

Negative problems only take us further away from the One who can solve any dilemma—our Lord Jesus Christ. Worry would have you believe there is no escape from this thing. But don't you believe it! Nothing could be further from the truth, for Christ has the power to overcome *any* situation that arises. In the negative-thinking attitude we have become a trapped victim of the enemy of despair. It is not difficult to become ensnared by the rope of depression that seems to be hanging about our neck.

Worry causes depression to become a way of life. We encounter real and imaginary problems that might greatly influence our everyday lives. Our thought processes can become clogged up, allowing worries to build up and causing us to feel as though life is useless and meaningless. Don't think this couldn't happen to you. It can! Perhaps it already has. Worry is an enemy. It should be understood for what it is—a negative element in our lives. Worry can depress the mind and spirit so severely that it can even cause physical illness.

There is no wonder that frustration comes from worry. Frustration and worry walk together, almost unnoticed, spreading unhappiness and misery all about. It is not until the harm is done that we become alarmed. When these two forces team up we need to take immediate notice of them. They are sending us a loud message, "There is an unmet need in your life." This warning should be heeded and tended to. To decode the full message sent by worry and frustration takes effort on our part. We must desire to understand what our spiritual nature is telling us.

Here are some truths we may receive when we look into the problem.

1. The unmet need you have is the lack of or the need for a closer personal relationship with Christ the Savior. Perhaps you have allowed your relationship with Him to slide a bit. Perhaps you must realize that Christ really

hasn't ever been a part of your life. Or perhaps you have neglected and been unwilling to let God be God.

2. There must be a real desire to set worry in its place, but you aren't sure how.

3. You must desire to do away with the negative and allow positive action to take place in your life.

4. You must choose your priorities. Who and what is of major importance to me? Is it my faith? My work? My heart's desires? My position in the community? Setting priorities is vital to a proper relationship with Christ.

There are other things that we might need to consider from the warnings worry sends our way.

1. What lessons have you learned from worry? Make a list of them.

2. Why is it important to face worry head on and not ignore its challenge to your spiritual well-being?

3. What kind of relationship to Christ did you have during these moments of worry?

4. How have you resolved the frustrations that result from worry and despair in your life?

Each of these questions is of equal importance in your understanding the heartaches that come from negative thinking. Now that we see worry as it is, we can begin to deal with it. God desires that we become aware of the need for change in our lives. He wants us to have a full life and a happier one built on full knowledge of His will for us.

Avoidable Worries

There are moments in our lives when we can avoid worry. Oftentimes our worry is brought on by unrealistic thinking. We create problems where there really aren't any at all. We begin to think that something "might happen" or "could happen." These thoughts give worry a place to build. Our imagination tends to lead us to extremes when it is not kept in check. The more we concentrate on the thing that bothers us, the more it becomes a reality. Soon it becomes a seemingly unconquerable problem all because it was nurtured and fed.

There is no need to look for trouble in your daily life. They come quickly enough as it is. You and I can sidestep these problems and avoid many moments of uneasiness and heartache if only we would ignore negative thoughts. It isn't easy to do and takes effort, but it can be done. You can rebuild your thought patterns and mental attitudes, but you must want to! I know a great deal about negative thinking, for it has plagued me for years. Allow me to share my findings with you.

I was a born worrier. (Well, not really! Worriers are self-made, not born. We make ourselves into worriers and want to be so, or else the feeling wouldn't exist!) When I was a young girl, the worry that I wasn't nearly as pretty or half as smart as the other children constantly plagued me. It seemed as though life was one problem after another. It also seemed as though I never felt happiness, only misery, for I had set my mind to the negative thoughts in life. I thought I had nothing to contribute to life.

No one had ever taught me or showed me how to have a positive attitude about anything. Encouragement was seldom offered me. I learned to dwell on the impossible instead of the possible. Thinking like this can only result in frustration, bitterness, and separation from God. It seemed as though there was no way to overcome the negative in my life. Every event was a major catastrophe until I encountered the love of Christ head on. With a true understanding of Jesus Christ as Savior and Lord, my life changed for the better!

It can be a struggle to re-establish the positive in your life, especially when you find it difficult to recognize it for what it is. It takes Christ foremost in your life to make things happen. A desire to grow and learn how to be a better person and the willingness to make changes in your life are accomplished through His guidance.

In the last few years I have made great strides in learning to overcome the negative. At times there is some backsliding on my part, but when this happens I just pick myself up and begin again. That is one of the wonderful blessings of being in Christ—I can start anew! Worry need not be my life style anymore, for I can trust Christ for *all* things in *all* areas of my life.

Unavoidable Worries

There are events about which we cannot help but worry to some degree. We may know that Christ can set aside all worries, but still we tend to be bothered by some.

It takes time for problems and heartaches to disappear. Few things change and disappear instantly, and time can heal and change those old attitudes that need changing. Everything that causes worry can become a stepping stone to maturity as children of God. Throughout life we learn whom to trust and believe in—Jesus. There is a certain realization that we as Christians need Christ at the control center of our lives. He knows those problems that beset us. He wants us to grow stronger and permits us to struggle to some degree in our lives. He knows, too, what we need to learn from each experience. Although Jesus teaches us not to concentrate on our worries, He doesn't want us to be flippant about them either. We are to do our part in overcoming adversities.

When unavoidable worries arise, there is often a feeling of frustration. We do not necessarily need to be beset by concern, but we can trust the Lord to show us the answers to our individual needs. Don't feel abnormal if a Christian brother or sister says to you, "It is a sin to worry!" Just rest in the peace that your frustration is known by Christ and between the two of you results will be seen in overcoming this trial. Don't feel guilty because someone has said, "You shouldn't worry or be fearful." It is normal to be concerned over our problems. Only God knows what there is in each lesson that arises. He teaches us directly— on a one-to-one basis. It is judgmental for another person to tell you that you "lack faith" or you "haven't given the problem over to God." They aren't helping you at all. They may even be causing you more problems by their "advice." *You* have to be a part of the cure, so that you can learn which treatment is most effective.

During these struggles the last thing we need is poor advice. Rather, they are times for encouraging and sharing kindness and love. Too often Christians seem to maintain a set of pat phrases about how to react to a given situation. Instead of replying with understanding, the Christian may tend to state one of these pat answers.

Thus, while we should support one another and bear one another's burdens, there still is a need to remain cautious in giving our advice. Who are we to judge the work that God does in the life of another Christian? We must be careful to avoid setting standards or establishing rules for other Christians to follow. We may help to unravel the work Christ is doing in the life of another person, but our words should always be chosen very carefully. Encouragement should be offered as an effort to build up others and reassure them in their Christian walk.

Our words may make a life-changing difference in the life of another. We can push them to the edge, or we can brighten their outlook on life. Since each of us faces turning points in our lives in which important choices are made, the words we hear can tear away at our faith or help it grow stronger, depending on the manner in which the words are spoken. Speak constructive thoughts of encouragement to your friends and loved ones.

Encouragement is necessary for living a positive life. The wise Christian shares love and faith in a manner that brings glory to Christ. It is Christ who knows the work that must be done to improve our lives, and we need to be encouragers of one another.

Symptoms of Worriers

UNEASINESS

When we notice a person who is ill at ease, we realize there are problems brewing. It doesn't take much to turn the restless attitudes into worry. Within a few moments a feeling of uneasiness can turn one's spirit inside out, causing turmoil to erupt.

People who are ill at ease usually have trouble making decisions. Even the most insignificant decision may weigh heavily on their shoulders. People can worry about a problem in such depth that it is impossible to make any decision at all, let alone the right decision. Surely God doesn't desire us to fall under such mental anguish that we cannot make the simplest of decisions.

NERVOUSNESS

Many of our modern-day worriers appear to be nervous people. Their life seems filled with little problems which seem to grow larger each day. For any number of reasons they have yet to shave the coarse edges off of life and gain a settled attitude.

Often people who claim to be nervous have not set priorities. They are not sure what they want or how to achieve goals, because they have not really committed themselves to a task. This is not to say that all people who encounter nervousness are without goals, for many do establish goals and achieve remarkable things. It is only that the nervous person has a difficult time finding peace. Peace is found in a calmness of spirit and a settled attitude. Most nervous people have yet to learn this.

For those who are easily upset or strung out by the problems of life, peace often eludes their grasp. From personal experience I can testify to numerous reasons for a feeling of being on edge. Small children, job insecurities, marriage difficulties, family problems, material needs, lack of self-esteem, health problems, and unbelief are but a few things that can cause problems. Any one or a combination of several of these can make one's life as shaky as a swinging bridge.

In my own life, low self-esteem has been my greatest battle. I had a feeling of insecurity because I believed that nothing I did was right. Negative feelings can quickly destroy a person's spirit if not overcome through Christ. As I came to understand that life is of value and that within myself there was potential to become a "vessel" for God's work, then spiritual strength and security became mine. Christ made the difference!

A careful study of the Scriptures demonstrates the importance of values in life. Christ considered us worthwhile, for He offered His life for our sins. What a great gift! Christ knows that each of us is unique in our own way. He gave us the priceless gift of eternal life through Him. My self-esteem grows stronger each day, for I sense His presence everywhere. I am secure in Christ.

There really need not be a prolonged struggle with nervousness. We need only gain the understanding that we cause most of our own problems. Have we trusted Christ *all* the time? Believing in Christ is one thing, but learning to trust Him at *all* times is still another. As this lesson is learned, you will see your trust grow. You might even find yourself wondering why you have not trusted Christ sooner.

Perhaps some of these ideas seem a little farfetched to you, especially if you have never struggled in this area. To the person whose heart seeks to be secure, these frustrations are very real. There is joy and comfort in learning about Christian commitment and then in following Christ daily. If you have not experienced this new-found freedom from nervousness and frustration, it may be difficult for you to understand my words. But if you seek to know the things of God, you too will find freedom. Life is complete only when we understand our position in Christ.

TENSION

Worry is often found to be a contributing factor to tension. The more serious the cause of worry, the worse the tension. Tension can pull at the muscles in the neck and back, causing discomfort and pain. Nothing seems to escape our attention as stress mounts. Worries pound in the head, and tensions in the body grow.

Notice that frustration often uses insignificant things to tear at us. Without any reason you might become jumpy and on edge. At the moment of its own choosing, tension lashes out. Frequently things are said or done to relieve stress; these things can later cause even more anguish and frustration. Although there is a need to express yourself and "get it off your chest," it is important to maintain control of your spirit.

Like many of the other areas we have examined, tension is the result of self-centeredness. Because minds and hearts are focused on ourselves, tension tugs away at us. We have allowed ourselves to become most important. We seldom find time to offer God a thought at all. We are too involved with our own lives and simply don't seek His guidance. We just don't want Christ to convict us of a need for change in our lives.

The list of problems created by worry grows. There are numerous reasons why worry has gained such a place of prominence in our lives. It is in realizing what worry seeks to do to our spiritual well-being that we can resist it. Countless frustrations can be put to rest as we see them in the light of godly standards. We should begin to view many of frustration's efforts as inconveniences. They shouldn't be allowed to harm our spiritual attitudes in the least. Most worries and frustrations can be eliminated by fully trusting and believing the words of the Scriptures. After all, there is nothing that we should allow to overpower us if we stand firmly rooted in God's Word.

Problems and Worries

Locate your pencil and paper for note taking. Make a list of things you worry about. Now ask yourself the following questions:

1. Why do I worry about these things?
2. How does worry change my problems?
3. Has there been any change in these problems as a result of worry?
4. Have I asked God to take charge of these problems?
5. Have I sought encouragement in overcoming these problems through a time of prayer and personal Scripture reading?
6. Do I really want these frustrations to leave me, or do I feed on them for excitement and meaning to life?

These questions may be difficult for you to answer. But try! Be honest and open with yourself. You might be surprised at the number of frustrations you can eliminate when you decide to hand them over to Christ. It isn't easy to admit you've made a mistake in handling life's problems, but it can be done. The first step is the hardest, because you have to see the error of your ways. This can be a little painful. But changes will not come until you want them to come. You have to take the first step—desire to turn aside the negative attitude and strive for a happier life.

Types of Worries

Have we given any thought to the things that tend to upset us? We encounter a variety of worries daily. There are times we might wonder, "Is there anything right with the world?" In this section of our chapter on worry we examine a few of the reasons we tend to worry. Don't be discouraged if some of these thoughts hit you in the face like a custard pie. They are such common problems that we sometimes allow them to become a part of our lives. Remember, this need not be so. We can set aside the major part of our worries and rest in the Lord.

MONEY

"Where will the money come from? There isn't enough money in the house to buy milk, let alone pay the bills!" Have you ever been in that situation? More likely than not you have. Almost all of us struggle with money or the lack of it.

Many times in the last twenty years of our marriage, things seemed almost impossible. Like most couples we have had some pretty hard times. When we needed something and wondered where the money would come from, we became troubled. The worry grew deeper with each passing day. Money, money, money, there is never enough of it! What can we do? The answer was, and still is, to allow our faith to work using God's resources.

Our worldly system is designed to run by the exchange of money. If we have nothing to exchange for goods, we may experience some very real heartaches. Frustration can be strong when we need something and can't afford it. Sometimes God tells us we must wait. You see, it is in waiting that we learn our need for Him. The more desperate our need, the more closely we listen to God. There are times when God says, "I'm sorry but you must learn the value of having money and spending it wisely." Whatever the reason God may tell us to wait, it is a good one. Christians should learn to accept God's response, whatever it may be.

Money is only of temporary importance and value. It cannot buy happiness, peace of mind, and a heart that is sensitive to God. Money can be a friend or an enemy. It can worry you or please you. When we learn the value of using what we have wisely, then we are usually blessed by more. Remember, God owns everything! That includes money, property, materialistic things; it all belongs to God. For the Christian the challenge is not to worry about money but to use it wisely as God directs. Ours is to share what we have, for it is in giving that we receive from God.

I would share with you the principle that as we share our finances with others, we receive an abundance of blessings. God does not always return an investment of money with additional money. There are, after all, many things that are far more important and lasting than money. Don't be deceived by the common teaching that you have to give to get, for that isn't always the way it works. It may be God will bless you with something far more precious than financial gain.

CARNALITY

Many Christian men and women have not realized that we are called upon to live a life style that is different from those who have not accepted Jesus Christ as Savior. We are to live in this world but not live by the standards of this world. Our Christian belief is not me first but Christ first! We then should place others second. We consider our own needs after that. That is the Master Plan. This has been set before us in the teachings of the Holy Bible, God's inspired Word. As we give, we receive the blessings Christ has awaiting us.

Understand the world speaks in carnal (or unspiritual) terms. "Take what you can get. Step on the other guy to get what you want. There is no hereafter, so do what you want today! Get whatever you want at any cost. Get all you can now, while you can." The carnal nature and the spiritual nature wage a constant battle to gain control of your thought processes. The person who thinks only of self-pleasure and self-satisfaction is never fully pleased. There is always more to gain or to have, and the carnal nature is always saying, "Me first!"

The spiritual nature seeks to draw us closer to a loving relationship with God. The natural (or carnal nature) has limited time for God. It surely doesn't intend to pursue a course which will result in holiness. Is there any wonder that worry and depression attach themselves to our carnal nature and often pull us to the depths of despair? There is no continual happiness in living outside of God. The pleasures of life are but fleeting moments without the love of God in our heart. True contentment comes from a loving relationship with our mighty God.

EMPTINESS

The person who struggles with an attitude of emptiness may face some very real problems. Worry can develop a life style that seems beset by loneliness and despair. Frustration grows stronger in our moments of wayward wanderings. Life may seem meaningless as we search for a reason to live.

People who are bothered by emptiness must search their hearts for answers. Why is life this way? What is it that I want from life? Where is my life headed? Why doesn't something change for the better? The list of questions seems to grow longer as time passes by. A life lacking direction can be deeply troubled. Allow me to share with you an example from my own life.

Forty years of my life quickly slipped by while I was searching, looking, and hunting for whatever it is that gives peace and happiness. Why it took me so long to understand God's plan for my life is still a great mystery to me. Perhaps my head was too hard and my spirit was calloused. But recently my heart became very sensitive to my need for God all of the time.

It was in learning the power of submission to the authority of the Holy Spirit that the emptiness turned into fruit-bearing. The years of frustration and emptiness have given way to a new life filled with completeness through the love of Jesus Christ.

Just yesterday an old acquaintance and I were talking. Her husband has been called into Christian service and they had come to Russellville for a visit. I have written her from time to time and shared some thoughts with her. As we were talking she said, "Do you know that you radiate a special glow?" I was surprised at her words. She continued, "I can see by your face that you have finally found peace within yourself. You are happy and it shows in your face. I am so glad to see you finally found happiness!"

My Christian friend's remarks sank deeply into my mind. How had she known of my struggles and heartaches? This woman had barely known me before she left here. After thinking about it, the reality that my life has become quite different since I began to write became clear. It has only been a few months since I learned the joy of sharing and being God's woman. It has given me my happiest moments. The moments of emptiness have disappeared and have been replaced by peace and joy within my soul. Frustration does not have control of my life any longer; Christ does. Christ has taken the emptiness and lack of involvement and sent them away to bother me no more. Christ will and can do the same for you, but you must want it to be so. It won't just happen, for it takes involvement on your part.

MATERIALISM

Why worry yourself with the desire for more materialistic things? That new house and car might not be as important as you think. There is a force within us that pulls at us, saying, "I've got to have this thing." It will indeed devour your spiritual nature and set the passions of your heart afire.

Materialism is the desire for an abundance of things. It will quickly separate you from God. We cannot do away with the needs we have for our earthly existence, but we can overcome the desires to have an overabundance of wealth and possessions. It is wise for us to recall that what we have, as children of God, really does belong to Him. It is in using what we have wisely that we are given more. Selfishness is ungodly.

We need to take stock of our lives on a regular basis. Having certain things is fine, but being reckless or foolish with our gains is unpleasing to God. God wants to give to us the things we can be trusted with, but only as we use them wisely. There is no need to worry over materialistic things, for in time they will all vanish and disappear. Why be frustrated over something that will not stand the test of time and eternity?

THE PAST

How often have you seen a person still struggling with an experience from the past? Ideas and memories that cause the past to be relived can cause heartaches. Something which occurred in the past cannot be changed. There is no need to let the past ruin the present or the future.

Past experiences should be just that—in the past. We are to leave behind our past mistakes and press on toward the future. Only as we forget those moments which cause us frustration and worry can we step forward reaching for a new tomorrow. Living with yesterday can hinder us from obtaining a spiritual maturity. The past can be painful, and as we focus our attention on events gone by we cannot see God in our life at all. Yesterday's problems can block our efforts to live for Christ today.

For those who are involved with problems of the past there are words of good cheer for you. Give that old problem away. Give it to Jesus. Jesus knows how to take care of it. You know your efforts haven't been that successful, so let Jesus show you what He can do. You will gain new insight as you begin to live for today, looking for a better way through complete knowledge of Jesus Christ. Our secret to overcoming is no secret at all. . . . Jesus Christ accepts responsibility for those who believe in Him. He can handle problems, past, present, and future with the greatest of ease. That within itself should give you great joy!

THE FUTURE

Almost as fruitless as worrying about the past is worrying about the future. There are countless numbers of men and women who struggle with the future. How will we live next month without help? Where will the children go to college? What will I do when I retire? Whom will I marry? There are many questions and only a limited number of answers.

Worry can ruin your future. It can oppress your spirit to the point that you find it difficult to reason for yourself. Worry renders you spiritually ineffective for the work of the Lord. As you worry, there is little room for God to maneuver in your life. Nothing seems to work out for the positive, because your mind is concerned with the negative.

Things change ever so rapidly. Technology seems to be growing at an alarming rate. Many people struggle with modern technology, such as nuclear warfare, the computer age, sophisticated modern medical advances, and so on. These can be genuine concerns, but some people allow them to unnecessarily complicate their lives. If they had as much concern about their commitment to their faith, the world surely would be an improved place. One seldom sees Christian people as committed to their beliefs as are those who endure the humility of protest, arrest, and persecution for worldly causes. Priorities need to be made and worry set aside whenever possible.

What will tomorrow bring? Who is to say? What can be done to change one minute of the future by worrying today? Not a thing! We have to reassure ourselves that tomorrow has been carefully planned by God. We are to be involved with living for today and be prepared to step forth into each new tomorrow.

While we are free to plan, we should not worry about the future. We must learn to give our lives over to Christ, one day at a time. The most meaningful days of our life are those we have dedicated to God. What more could we want?

Worry about the future? No, indeed! The secret to abundant life is in giving each day to the Lord. In the mornings, begin your day by saying, "Lord, I dedicate this day to You. Do whatever You wish with me." Do that and watch what happens! There is no greater joy than serving the Lord! Your future is secure in Him; there is nothing to fear. Each day He will take your positive contributions in life and use them to further your Christian maturity. The challenge of each new tomorrow need not be, "What will become *of* me?" The challenge can be, "What will Christ do *through* me?" The Christ-centered life is often filled with moments of quiet happiness. Worry need not lead to frustration, for through Jesus Christ our burdens can become lighter.

Thinking of the future should lead us to experiencing joy through Christ. Only He gives life a real purpose!

Remedy for Worry

Enough has been said about worry for a while. Let's consider the steps we can take to eliminate it from our lives. We will want to develop an in-depth comprehension of the positive and negative sides of worry. Next we consider the biblical solution to the source of worry, which can erupt into frustration. Get out your notebook, Bible, and pen, and we will make some important notes on overcoming worry.

Turn with me to chapter 6 of Matthew. We will begin reading in verse 25 and read through verse 34.

"Therefore I tell you, do not worry about your life, what you will eat or drink; or about your body, what you will wear. Is not life more important than food, and the body more important than clothes? Look at the birds of the air; they do not sow or reap or store away in barns, and yet your heavenly Father feeds them. Are you not much more valuable than they? Who of you by worrying can add a single hour to his life?

"And why do you worry about clothes? See how the lilies of the field grow. They do not labor or spin. Yet I tell you that not even Solomon in all his splendor was dressed like one of these. If that is how God clothes the grass of the field, which is here today and tomorrow is thrown into the fire, will he not much more clothe you, O you of little faith? So do not worry, saying, 'What shall we eat?' or 'What shall we drink?' or 'What shall we wear?' For the pagans run after all these things, and your heavenly Father knows that you need them. But seek first his kingdom and his righteousness, and all these things will be given to you as well. Therefore do not worry about tomorrow, for tomorrow will worry about itself. Each day has enough trouble of its own" (NIV).

Let's take a close look at these important verses. In the first paragraph (verses 25 through 27) we learn some important truths about life.

1. Make a note of the information Jesus gives you about life in these verses.
2. How does this information compare to the teaching He shares about the birds?
3. What does God consider our value to be in your thinking?
4. Can we add anything of value to life by unwarranted worry?
5. Why?

Isn't it amazing what Jesus' words have taught us on the subject of life! Now let's concentrate on verses 28 through 34.

6. Why are we often preoccupied by what we wear and what we have?
7. What does Jesus want us to understand on the subject of clothing?
8. How concerned should we be for our daily needs according to these verses?
9. What advice is found in verse 34?
10. How can following this advice change your way of thinking?

Worry need not overcome us, for Jesus has said so. He has given us the reassurance that we are of value to Him. He teaches us that we are far more important than any of God's creatures, and He tells us not to worry. Worry doesn't gain anything. As we worry we place the love He has for us on hold. When we reject the peace and security Jesus offers us, we are telling Him, "I'm not sure this problem will work itself out to my advantage. Perhaps if I show more concern and work harder, it will work out to my benefit and everything will be fine."

To really set worry aside we must allow the Lord to work freely. If we limit our faith as it seeks to work in our lives we will see only limited results to our problems. We need to recall the security given us through Christ. In Hebrews 13:5, 6 we pick up some additional information on the blessings which come from Christ. As we receive a full understanding of our position in Christ, we can easily overcome worry and frustration. "Keep your lives free from the love of money and be content with what you have, because God has said, 'Never will I leave you; never will I forsake you.' So we say with confidence, 'The Lord is my helper; I will not be afraid. What can man do to me?' "

Do you see what the Scriptures are trying to tell us? Nothing can overcome us for a prolonged period of time when God is our Helper. He has given us top priority in caring and sharing for us, because He is our Lord and Savior. Don't allow worry and frustration to snatch Jesus' gifts away from you. There is no need to be afraid or worry, for there is nothing that Christ cannot overcome. We belong to Him.

What security we have as we realize that it is Christ who stands as our Warrior! Without Him we are in a weakened state, but with the Lord at our side, there is nothing that can pull us apart from His safety. I am His and He is mine.

Let's look at Philippians 4:4–6 and read together this message of encouragement sent from the Lord above. "Rejoice in the Lord always. I will say it again: Rejoice! Let your gentleness be evident to all. The Lord is near. Do not be anxious about anything, but in everything, by prayer and petition, with thanksgiving, present your requests to God" (NIV). Look at the words of wisdom in these verses.

1. There is reason to rejoice always, for the Lord is near.
2. We have nothing to be anxious about. The Lord will control our fears and problems as we submit to His authority.
3. Prayer will help us overcome even the most adverse of circumstances.
4. God will act on our requests for help, but they must first be made to Him.
5. God is listening and is ready to act instantly on our behalf to relieve us of many of the worries and frustrations we now encounter.

Those are real words of encouragement for me. I hope they are for you too. Now read aloud verse 7 and listen to the words of hope. "And the peace of God, which transcends all understanding, will guard your hearts and your minds in Christ Jesus." Now I call that reason to be excited. The peace of God will guard our hearts and minds in Christ Jesus. My dear friends, if God is allowing our hearts and minds to be guarded by His Son, surely there is nothing to fear. That should give you a special peace and happiness and surely a reason to get excited about your faith. Worry is defeated the very moment you realize your position in Christ.

Worry can be forgotten and ignored. We are free to pick up our lives and move out in faith, understanding that it is Christ who carries us forth each day of our lives. Nothing anyone can do will separate us from the love Christ has for us. Let us renew our vow to love Christ in a true spirit of love. We will be happy we did!

QUESTIONS

1. What does worry accomplish?

2. How often do you worry, resulting in an attitude of frustration?

3. How does worry add to the daily pressures of life?

4. Why does worry tend to draw you away from God?

5. How can worry be set aside?

6. How does God expect you to deal with worry when it comes?

7. Why is it useless to worry about the future?

8. How can worry interfere with the master plan God has prepared for the Christian?

9. What is the value of encouragement?

10. Locate five Scriptures that can be used as a source of encouragement during troubled times. Write them in your notebook.

11. What are some types of worries that are familiar to you?

12. What do you consider to be the most important information set before you in Matthew 6:25–34?

13. Have you learned to trust God with your worries?

14. What advice can you give another person that might encourage them during a period of worry and stress?

15. Locate four Scriptures that concentrate on the subject of worry. Share them with a friend.

chapter
6

how to deal
with frustration

*Maturity begins to grow when you
can sense your concern for others
outweighing your concern for
yourself.*

John MacNaughton

We are involved in a study of both mind and spirit as viewed in the spiritual realm. We have traveled a long distance to gain an understanding of frustration. Our first steps were taken toward the realization of how frustration seeks to work in our lives. We then learned how frustration tries to burden us using attitudes of worry, frustration, anger, anxiety, and all those other negative ideas that seek to separate us from the love and security of Christ, our Lord. We now come to the best of the study—the realization that frustration is readily overcome with reasonable effort.

We can use three powerful weapons to defeat the attitudes that seek to isolate us from Christ. First, we can use the common sense God has given us by simply saying "no" to frustrations. Second, the Bible is a very effective tool and weapon against any force that seeks to draw us away from the God, who will instruct and encourage us as we read it. It should be the Christian's textbook for life. It is a source of strength to those who seek God's guidance. Third and by no means least, is the power of the Holy Spirit, who lives within each believer. Frustration has no other choice than to leave us, for by the Holy Spirit's power we can and will defeat any force seeking to steal us away from the love of the Father. The Holy Spirit waits to be our Warrior in the battle of life. When asked and not hindered by us, He will defeat the enemy quickly!

In composing this important chapter, I realized that we need to be aware of the steps to take that can overcome frustration. We will then move on to a *practical application* of how to overcome frustration. We then review Scriptures of importance that serve as encouragers.

Step One:
Our Relationship with Christ

Why has frustration come into my life? This is the first question you need to ask yourself. *Examine your mind and heart* to determine why you have become "bogged down" with worry and frustration. *Something* has happened to set you off of your normal routine.

Understand that frustration is a common occurrence. Do not allow it to have ground to build upon. Stop it before it gets started. You see frustration's results because you wander off of the path you normally travel and seek a different path. Something or someone has caused a temporary distraction, and your attention is focused elsewhere. You may have been walking a consistent walk with Christ, and then something happened to send you slightly astray. Now you are encountering some frustration.

Your first step toward understanding this problem is to look at your relationship with Christ. Determine where you stand in Him. If you are in constant contact and are maintaining a meaningful relationship with the Savior, frustration will soon fade away. But if you have allowed your daily walk to slip into some of your old unlovely habits, then you can be sure that frustration will linger a while. You see, frustration can't get a full grasp on us when we focus our time and efforts on Christ's desire for our lives. There really need be no major problems from frustrations. We need experience only minor delays from time to time. A close relationship with Christ protects us from many of the hazards of negative living. That should be encouraging news for you.

Frustration can't keep step with the power of Christ in your spirit. If you do encounter a problem with frustration, then it must be dealt with through the might and power of Christ. You cannot defeat the forces that seek to draw you into a trap of despair on your own. This is one of the greatest reasons each of us has a need for Christ as Lord and Savior of our lives. There is no need to wrestle alone, for Christ desires to help us. That is part of God's divine plan for a complete life; the Holy Spirit is our Guide, our Helper, and our Companion.

Step Two:
Acknowledge the Problem

It is necessary to acknowledge frustration and its presence in your life. When you acknowledge the awareness of a problem, you can begin to deal with it. Before frustration grasps your spirit and gains control of your common sense, acknowledge that something is wrong and you need help.

What you are experiencing is not unusual. Remember that even the apostle Paul had his moments of frustration. He openly acknowledged this in his letter to the Romans. Turn with me to chapter 7 and watch as Paul unravels his frustration before us. Let's read verses 19 and 20 from the New King James Version. "For the good that I will to do, I do not do; but the evil I will not do, that I practice. Now if I do what I will not to do, it is no longer I who do it, but sin that dwells in me."

Paul is giving us extensive information not only about his problem but his attitude about the problem. You see our attitude has a great deal to do with the effects of frustration. Paul understands the necessity of setting his life back on the right track. He does not fail to acknowledge his problem or openly state its existence. See what Paul says in verse 19.

1. The good which he sought to do, he did not. How frustrating! Paul was aware of the value of doing what was right. Yet he struggled with what to do.
2. The evil he sought to avoid attached itself to him like a fly on a jar of honey. It was attracted to him, because he was in a state of uncertainty and indecision.
3. Paul's heart might have said, "Turn away from evil," but yet he was still tempted to do it. Paul had his hands full.

Now look at verse 20. Paul wanted us to understand the wrong that results from evil desires. He knew he had to be careful or sin would result from his trials. Each of us slips from time to time, even when we try not to. It is part of our nature to struggle. The worse the trial, the stronger our need, and the more we need the loving Savior. These moments illustrate why it is so necessary for us to allow Christ to be our Lord and Savior. We cannot save ourselves. We need Jesus! While we can resist and turn away from evil, the Lord Jesus Christ will carry us through each trial safely.

Paul calls to our attention one of his greatest messages. Read verses 24 and 25. "O wretched man that I am! Who will deliver me from this body of death? I thank God—through Jesus Christ our Lord! So then, with the mind I myself serve the law of God, but with the flesh the law of sin" (NKJV). He then carries his thought just a bit further into chapter 8, verses 1 through 3. "There is therefore now no condemnation to those who are in Christ Jesus, who do not walk according to the flesh, but according to the Spirit. For the law of the Spirit of life in Christ Jesus has made me free from the law of sin and death. For what the law could not do in that it was weak through the flesh, God did by sending His own Son in the likeness of sinful flesh, on account of sin: He condemned sin in the flesh" (NKJV).

Paul had quite a bit to say in these verses. These truths should give us considerable insight into life's problems. Why not take your notebook and write the key thoughts down for later reference? The great apostle Paul understood his need for Jesus Christ. Ask yourself these questions and write your responses.

1. Do I really understand my need for Christ?
2. Is He part of my life every moment of the day, or do I just call on Him in emergency situations?

Your answers might surprise you. I know mine did me. Our honest evaluations often show us our need for a change.

It is only as we acknowledge our problems and recall in whom the solution is found that we can become true victors over frustration. God wants us to live a life that is victorious and joy-filled. Acknowledgment of a problem brings full awareness of the situation. It allows frustration to rise to the surface, so that it might be fully recognized and dealt with.

Step Three:
Fear Not

This step is more difficult for some of us than it will be for others. Accept the idea that frustration can lead to an emotional problem. Recall, Christian, that "you have not received a spirit of slavery leading to fear again, but you have received a spirit of adoption" (Romans 8:15 NAS).

Frustration need not control your life. Accept the responsible position that something is emotionally rubbing you in the wrong direction. Bear in mind this difficulty need not enslave you, for Romans 8:15 gives you a special assurance. You need not fear!

"You were bought with a price; do not become slaves of men" (1 Corinthians 7:23 NAS). Don't allow any person or any situation to overpower your spiritual nature. Christ paid the price for you and me when He bore our sins and problems on the cross. Christ has freed you, so that you need not suffer from frustration or mental anguish at any moment. He wants you to be filled and happy, not distraught. Christian friend, please understand that frustration need not have an overwhelming effect on your life. In fact, worry and frustration have no need to bind our spirits in any manner. Frustration is running a bluff. It wants to disturb your peace of mind and godly spirit.

Only as we give emotions their way and allow them to take charge of the situation can we be defeated. The more I study the areas of frustration that we encounter, the more convinced I am that I need not give way to them in the least. We should be in charge of our lives; God has given us the authority to make our own choices. What will be *your* choice? Surely God means for you to stand fast and say "no." We are to resist evil, and it will turn away! It's your decision and mine! We are free to live an abundant life, filled with a full measure of God's love. By saying "no" to frustration, we can walk on with our heads held high. To say "yes" to frustration is to resist the Holy Spirit's offer of guidance. We choose for ourselves which path to take.

Here are some thoughts for you from the Scriptures. Consider what God wants you to learn through them.

1. "Prove yourselves doers of the word, and not merely hearers who delude themselves" (James 1:22 NAS).

2. "Therefore, to one who knows the right thing to do, and does not do it, to him it is sin" (James 4:17 NAS).

3. "Therefore, gird your minds for action, keep sober in spirit, fix your hope completely on the grace to be brought to you at the revelation of Jesus Christ" (1 Peter 1:13 NAS).

4. "Submit therefore to God. Resist the devil and he will flee from you. Draw near to God and He will draw near to you" (James 4:7, 8a NAS).

5. "Then the Lord knows how to rescue the godly from temptation, and to keep the unrighteous under punishment for the day of judgment" (2 Peter 2:9 NAS).

There are great words of comfort and instruction in the Scriptures. As we acknowledge the reality of the problems at hand, we can free ourselves of the strain and stress we are encountering. Sounds simple, doesn't it? Well, it is! It all depends on our readiness to trust the Lord and confess our need.

Step Four:
Think Positive, Fight Back

Think! What is this thing doing to my health? Am I willing to allow this situation to break me and bend my life at its convenience? More than likely, you are not. That is the way it should be. Fight back, and don't allow frustration to have a free hand in your life.

Think positive! Frustration never reflects love or goodness. It only limits our vision. It tends to make us look only at our own needs and forget about everything else. While some frustration cannot be avoided, the majority of it can. Look at these thoughts of encouragement.

1. "Therefore, since we have so great a cloud of witnesses surrounding us, let us also lay aside every encumbrance, and the sin which so easily entangles us, and let us run with endurance the race that is set before us, fixing our eyes on Jesus, the author and perfecter of faith, who for the joy set before Him endured the cross, despising the shame, and has sat down at the right hand of the throne of God. For consider Him who has endured such hostility by sinners against Himself, so that you may not grow weary and lose heart" (Hebrews 12:1–3 NAS).

How about it, Christian friend? What does this tell you about our abilities to overcome frustration and adversity? Let us begin to claim the promises and wisdom given us by God and allow God to show us a better way. Do we see the importance of this passage? We must fix our eyes on Jesus, run with endurance our race, lay aside every encumbrance. We've been living in the negative when we allow frustration to sneak in and take hold. We surely should be thankful and give praise for the truth of Hebrews 12:1–3.

2. "Take care, brethren, lest there should be in any one of you an evil, unbelieving heart, in falling away from the living God" (Hebrews 3:12 NAS).

This verse asks the question, "Do I really have a believing heart? Do I believe Jesus for every part of my life?" It is vital that we understand our relationship to Christ and to let Him take charge of our lives. We should never allow any situation to make us emotionally or physically ill because we are not secure in our beliefs. It is our responsibility to grow and mature, so that our lives can blossom and radiate the beauty of Christ in us.

3. "Do not throw away your confidence, which has a great reward" (Hebrews 10:35 NAS).

Once again we see the necessity of gaining our confidence through Christ. How can we, as children of God, not grow more confident each day knowing in whom we believe. The answer is to secure the confidence and trust for life through full knowledge of Jesus' gift for us— salvation and eternal life through the love offering of Himself.

It grieves me that many who will read these words have no knowledge of the Scriptures. If this is true of you, please begin to read your Bible. Learn more about your faith. There is so much to life when it is lived in the positive faith. There is great happiness to gain in reading the New Testament and learning how great a blessing it is to be a member of the family of God.

Step Five: Confess Your Need

Confess that you cannot handle your situation alone. Confess you have made mistakes. If you have sinned, confess that too. God will relieve you of a heavy burden and free you from frustration. Just because you are frustrated does not necessarily mean there has been sin in your life. It only means that you need to ask for guidance from the Lord.

Until you learn to stop pushing the blame onto someone else or another circumstance, you cannot set frustrations aside and forget them. They will continue to be bothersome until properly dealt with. As you begin to accept the responsibilities for your decisions and actions, then you can unchain yourself from the burdens that have manifested in your spirit. Pride often keeps people from setting the wrongs right in their life, and their ego can become so inflated that, no matter what the problem, someone else is always to blame. Misdirected pride can cause your spirit to be almost totally insensitive to the call of God. Living with a worldly set of standards can also result in cutting off fellowship with other Christians as well as losing touch with God. The greater your pride, the less likely you might feel the need to associate with other Christians. You might feel as though other Christians have nothing to offer you. Do you see how important a proper relation can be? Friends confess their needs not only to one another but to Christ.

Frankly, some of us tend to think confession isn't really a necessary part of our lives. After all, "God knows my problems and weaknesses." Confession is good for us to speak not only to God but to ourselves. It makes us aware that we have need to improve our weak points. Confession also opens the line of communication between us and the Lord. The lack of accepting the responsibility for our deeds allows the line of communication we have with the Lord to become clogged. Finally, there is no communication at all. If frustration has caused you to sin, confess it to God. Without confession we soon cut ourselves off from the Lord, for we lose interest in things that are spiritual. If we feel guilty, it may isolate us from God, causing us to flee from Him. Confession of problem areas keeps the slate clean and allows our spirit to be in tune to God's instructions.

SCRIPTURES ABOUT CONFESSION

David as the writer of the book of Psalms displays a unique quality. His prayers were both meaningful and practical. He prayed from the heart to a listening God, our God, for all of his needs. Turn with me to Psalm 51, verses 1 through 4, for a close look at a meaningful prayer of confession, petition, and praise. "Have mercy on me, O God, according to your unfailing love; according to your great compassion blot out my transgressions. Wash away all my iniquity and cleanse me from my sin. For I know my transgressions, and my sin is always before me. Against you, you only, have I sinned and done what is evil in your sight, so that you are proved right when you speak and justified when you judge" (NIV).

David's prayer teaches us some important lessons about confession and prayer. First, David got to the point. He asked for mercy and forgiveness of his sin. He made no excuses for his wrong attitudes or his sin. He accepted the responsibility for his own actions. Then he asked to have his sin blotted out and his iniquity cleansed. He knew God would forgive him and claimed the right to ask forgiveness and received it. He understood that he had done wrong and confessed it to God, knowing that God was already fully aware of what he had done. David confessed to God and honestly sought to repent (turn away) from the wrong he had done. That is the proper way to receive forgiveness. Ask and receive it freely from God.

"Create in me a pure heart, O God, and renew a steadfast spirit within me. Do not cast me from your presence or take your Holy Spirit from me. Restore to me the joy of your salvation and grant me a willing spirit, to sustain me" (vv. 10–12 NIV). Notice that David was sincere in his confession. He sought full restoration of his position. He understood the importance of a complete and full relationship with God. David loved God. He had a heart that feared God. David feared continual sin and its destructive pattern, so he freed himself from the frustrations sin causes. He asked God for help.

Surely, the numerous examples of prayer and petition throughout the book of Psalms are a living example of God's continuing love for His people. David finally became a great servant of God as he gained a submissive spirit toward God.

You and I can be used of God much like David when we truly seek to live a life that concentrates on godliness. We have a tremendous challenge before us, my Christian friend. We have the privilege of serving Christ as He calls us to aid Him. But to do so, we must confess and be sensitive to God's call. With confession comes the privilege to mature in Christ. The privilege to step forth and walk in a manner worthy of our calling should thrill your soul. For it is in the calling which Christ Jesus gives to each person who believes in Him that true happiness and peace are found.

1 John 1:9, 10 says, "If we confess our sins, He is faithful and just to forgive us our sins and to cleanse us from all unrighteousness. If we say that we have not sinned, we make Him a liar, and His word is not in us" (NKJV).

The word *if* is the key to the truth in these two verses. "If" places the responsibility on us to admit there is a problem. When we confess that frustration has taken hold of our common sense and better judgment, then something can be done about it. To really eliminate a problem we must admit it exists. Our true friends understand when there is frustration in our life. They will want to help us eliminate it. After all, they do love us.

I hope you have gained strength in the understanding of confession in the area of frustration.

Step Six:
Make a Positive Decision

Now that you have traveled this far, allow me to tell you the worst is behind you. From this point on you will want to begin to concentrate on the good element that is part of your life. Remember you have the divine guidance of the Lord in your life. As a Christian you are expected to draw on that power. God is so good! He wants good things for those who love Him and trust Him. Decide that you will look forward to the glory of Christ, not over your shoulder at past frustrations. Decide you want God's goodness for your life.

Be positive in thought, recalling that God will supply your needs. You must give Him a fair chance by reaching for the good things in life that He has held in store for those who believe in Him. Think on Jesus! There is no more positive thought or action than trusting and believing in Jesus. Second, allow Him the full freedom to work in your life.

Look at the following verses as a source of encouragement:

1. "And my God shall supply all your needs according to His riches in glory in Christ Jesus" (Philippians 4:19 NAS).

2. "I can do all things through Him who strengthens me" (Philippians 4:13 NAS).

3. "And the peace of God, which surpasses all comprehension, shall guard your hearts and your minds in Christ Jesus. Finally, brethren, whatever is true, whatever is honorable, whatever is right, whatever is pure, whatever is lovely, whatever is of good repute, if there is any excellence and if anything worthy of praise, let your mind dwell on these things. The things you have learned and received and heard and seen in me, practice these things; and the God of peace shall be with you" (Philippians 4:7–9 NAS).

4. "Set your mind on the things above, not on the things that are on earth" (Colossians 3:2 NAS).

5. "Whatever you do in word or deed, do all in the name of the Lord Jesus, giving thanks through Him to God the Father" (Colossians 3:17).

6. "Devote yourselves to prayer, keeping alert in it with an attitude of thanksgiving; praying at the same time for us as well, that God may open up to us a door for the word" (Colossians 4:2a, b NAS).

These words of encouragement should give your heart plenty of reason to rejoice. Do you see the key in overcoming frustration? It is in getting outside of yourself. Set aside your problems and worries and focus your attention on helping others! You will be surprised at the difference this attitude will make in your life. "Others first, me last!" Sounds frightening, but it really isn't. It works! When you think of others and are sensitive to their needs, frustration will quickly die away. You cannot remain frustrated for a prolonged period of time when you are helping someone else.

Involvement in life is the key to a filled life. Don't be just an onlooker, be a participant in living each day. Be enthusiastic about each day. The Christian life was never meant to be listless and unexciting. It was meant to be filled with love that reaches out and shares with all people. It was meant to be involved. Christian friend, Christ was involved with people wherever He went. Recognize the fact that being a part of life is caring, as our Lord Jesus Christ cared. We carry on His work, for we are chosen for a task. Paul said, "For we are God's fellow workers; you are God's field, God's building" (1 Corinthians 3:9 NIV).

We are people sent forth to be involved in the task of sharing Jesus Christ. That takes involvement. That takes preparation. That takes freedom from worry, anxiety, depression, frustration, and fear. It takes a commitment on our part to allow our Lord to mold our spirits into something beautiful and radiant, into servants of the Lord. Only by reaching forth can we share our faith. That's what our lives are to be— living, sharing examples of deep-seated faith in Christ.

Even if you are somewhat hindered by a physical condition, you still have a gift to share. Don't allow frustration to whisper, "You have nothing to offer anyone, let alone God." Nothing, absolutely nothing, could be further from the truth. God has a unique plan for each of us, and we are to learn it, expand its use, and share it with the full knowledge that God will do whatever work He wants done through us. Press on, good friend, in Christ, and allow the Lord to show you the way. Remember these meaningful Scriptures, "Therefore humble yourselves under the mighty hand of God, that He may exalt you in due time, casting all your care upon Him, for He cares for you" (1 Peter 5:6, 7 NKJV). What a blessing He has given us in loving us and allowing us to share His love in return.

Christian friend, Jesus taught us that we are to love others as we love ourselves. The reason many frustrations enter our lives is because we have neglected to follow this great commandment. We elude the responsibility to share Christian love. As frustration comes, it isolates our thoughts and limits our response to love others. We think only of ourselves or the problem before us and refuse to share God's great love with others.

The second greatest joy of the Christian life should be in sharing what you are, what you have, and your faith with others. There is nothing for frustration to do when you are occupied with loving in the manner that Jesus taught. Frustration fades away when love is shared. Love is an unselfish giving and sharing. Frustration cannot hold up without selfish support. True godly love eliminates many of life's frustrations. Loving, Christian concern for others is necessary for the well-balanced Christian life. Believe and trust. Share and love. Those are lessons Jesus taught time and time again. Apply them each day to your life.

Remember, frustrations may still come but not those major frustrations you once encountered. Frustration's tactics are thwarted when you understand why it enters into your life and how to deal with it. Recall, we mentioned the fact that frustration need not be an enemy; well, that's true. It can become a friend if handled properly. Frustration can be used for our benefit when we allow God to instruct us in how to deal with it. It can clearly show us that need we have to grow in the knowledge of Christ in us. Frustrations can turn to joy, because it is through understanding how to deal with misunderstandings, worry, stress, weariness, sorrow, anger, and the many other symptoms that Christ is glorified. Frustration can be a tool to help focus our needs on the power of God. It is in moments of distress that we need only confess our inadequacies for help to be sent our way. God turns even the worst possible of circumstances to work for good with His divine powers and grace. Frustration can be a friend when we let it point the way to our need for further involvement with our Father.

A Promise

"Commit your way to the Lord, trust also in Him, and He will do it. And He will bring forth your righteousness as the light, and your judgment as the noonday. Rest in the Lord and wait patiently for Him; do not fret because of him who prospers in his way, because of the man who carries out wicked schemes. Cease from anger, and forsake wrath; do not fret, it leads only to evildoing. For evildoers will be cut off, but those who wait for the Lord, they will inherit the land. Yet a little while and the wicked man will be no more; and you will look carefully for his place, and he will not be there. But the humble will inherit the land, and will delight themselves in abundant prosperity" (Psalm 37:5–11 NAS).

The promise given us here is that as we commit our ways to the Lord many things will begin to change in our lives. The promised desires of our heart might have become different now, for as we become a vital part of giving and sharing our priorities change. For some, this may be difficult to understand. For others who have experienced it, this truth has become a certainty. The things of the world do not hold the importance or position they once did as we strive to be His person.

Commitment allows you to see the things which really are important in life and view them with a standard that comes from our Lord. We still have desires and needs, but now our sense of reason and depth of understanding show us which things are really important. The things which are right for us are the things that God will give to us. Because Christians make a full commitment of their lives does not mean they will live in a state of poverty. Only God knows what is best for each of us. Ours is to trust Him for all things. We can remain joyful, knowing "My God shall supply all your needs according to His riches in glory in Christ Jesus" (Philippians 4:19 NAS).

Commit your life and your spirit entirely to the Lord Jesus Christ and watch the abundance of the Christian life come your way.

It isn't as difficult as you might think to give up some old habits. The fact is that, in giving up the unpleasant parts of life, you gain a more meaningful walk with Christ the Lord. Mental frustrations might tell you that you cannot change yourself to follow Christ's example, but this is foolishness. Following Christ on a moment-by-moment basis will allow you to live life to the fullest. For it is in your loving commitment to Christ that you become aware of the need to encourage others.

Our Protector

"Be anxious for nothing, but in everything by prayer and supplication with thanksgiving let your requests be made known to God. And the peace of God, which surpasses all comprehension, shall guard your hearts and your minds in Christ Jesus" (Philippians 4:6, 7 NAS).

These words should stir your spirit and fill you with a special blessing from our Lord. We have so much going for us as children of light (see Ephesians 5:8) that we cannot fail to win over frustration or any other enemy. We do, after all is said and done, have the ultimate victory through our Lord and Savior Jesus Christ.

Jesus Christ is our Protector, our Savior, our Friend, and ever so much more. It has become a prayer burden of mine that most people have yet to understand this. Christ is a personal Lord and Savior! He knows each of us personally. He sees our strengths and weaknesses and still He loves us. He wants us to understand the importance of knowing Him on a personal level, just as you become acquainted with anyone else. The major difference is that Jesus the Lord is *our* Savior.

There is so much confidence and peace to be found in knowing that Christ cares. Think for a moment about your feelings toward Christ. Now answer the following questions:

1. How real is Jesus Christ to me?
2. Have I really understood the importance of Christ's teachings as seen in the New Testament?
3. Do I really believe the teachings of Christ?
4. Have I really thought through the life of Christ to see what He has done for me?
5. As a Christian, have I truly had a personal encounter or do I have heart knowledge of Christ as Lord and Savior?
6. Do I truly believe that Christ can save me from sin and evil? Why?
7. What steps have I taken to allow Christ to be my Lord, my Protector, my Savior, and my Guide through all the days of my life?
8. What kind of commitment have I made as a Christian to be a living part of Christ's ministry here on earth?

Jesus Christ is fully aware of the attitude of your heart. He knows your feelings as no one else does. He does not turn His help away from you, child of God, because you resist His ways or neglect to follow His example. Our Protector, Jesus Christ, still gives His all for you and me.

You should not overlook that fact. What you and I need to do is establish better habits and attitudes in living by His standards. The closer we draw to our Protector, the safer we will be, for nothing can overpower the One who loves us so greatly.

Good Habits

Using the steps we have discussed, combined with a regular time of Bible reading and prayer, will allow some great changes to take place in your life. As you begin to develop the habit of reading the Bible for gaining wisdom, insight, knowledge, and direction, you will begin to grow and mature in faith.

Determine in your mind and heart that you really do want to read the Bible. Allow yourself a few moments to do so whenever possible. You might even carry a small New Testament with you. You will be amazed at how often you will use it and how glad you will be to have it. There is nothing weak or foolish about reading a Bible in public, so do it! In fact, we need more men and women who are willing to stand strong in their faith and show others the way to search for Christ. Be brave enough to set an example for others. Even five minutes of Scripture reading per day can make a difference. You will never experience the joy of the abundant life until you make your own commitment to learn what it is. And it is found in a deeper understanding of Jesus Christ and His love for you. Get excited about your opportunity to read the Word of God. It will expand your views and enlighten your heart.

Remember to pray! You can pray almost anywhere and at any time: riding on a subway, driving on a trip, flying in an airplane, at school, while shopping. Oh, by all means in church, and don't think it's foolish to pray at bedtime. Christianity needs to encourage prayer. When God's people pray, wonderful things happen. Prayer gives us strength to live. It makes a vital difference in daily living. It lends courage and gives peace to troubled spirits. In prayer there is an opportunity to praise, offer thanks, ask for others, petition, and ask forgiveness. It is also the perfect time to quietly listen for God. God wants to maintain a close relationship with us. We are, after all, His adopted children through His Son Jesus Christ. Prayer is a necessity in the Christian's life.

It all sounds so simple, doesn't it? Well, it is! When you begin to put all the pieces of the puzzle of life together, things fit together nicely through God's direction. Nothing is left out to complete this puzzle, for God wants us to be filled with His peace and joy. You and I really do need Christ! It's true, none of us can function wholly and perfectly without His loving guidance. The easiest part of all is that the Holy Spirit lives within us, as we who have accepted Christ know. When we neglect Christ's gifts and help, then we are only robbing ourselves of a special joy. Be glad! Be positive! Be aware that we must walk with our eyes focused on Him, for only He can keep us safe!

When I first became aware that with my Christian life came certain responsibilities, I did not know how I could carry through living in such a manner in order to achieve God's plan. I needed to understand that Christ makes life special. He will and does show us the way to gain a perfect peace and trust by walking with our heads held high and allowing our hearts to be filled with His goodness.

Christ takes the old, unlovely parts from my life and slowly changes them into something far better. He then takes hold of the situation and shows me a better way to live. He demonstrates time and time again the positive attitudes of life when learned through Him. He gives me reason to rejoice! He allows me to see that, with all my imperfections and flaws, I am somebody special. He wants you to know that about yourself too! None of us are rejected by Him; we only reject Him because our own standards are not His standards. He doesn't consider us hopeless and without a chance. He wants to show you a better way! The way is found in Him.

I am glad that I have learned not to trust those inadequate feelings of frustration and nothingness any longer. For Christ, my Savior, gives me a "newness of spirit." Christ gives me a special reason to live my life for Him and be glad that I am myself. Loving ourselves is important, and that is one of the greatest lessons Christ ever taught me.

Humble Yourself

By using our common sense and understanding, the steps we take in overcoming frustrations give us the correct footing to step forward for Christ. There are two or three things which I have saved for you until the end of this chapter as a sort of spiritual bonus.

All of the advice in the world and all the words in the Scriptures can be useless to you unless you *humble yourself.* Humble yourself before God. "Therefore humbly submit to God's strong hand, so that at the proper time He may exalt you. Cast every worry you have upon Him, because He cares for you." (1 Peter 5:6, 7 Williams). When there is a need for God's loving guidance, humble yourself before Him. It isn't as difficult as it sounds. Your pride is useless if you cannot function properly as God's child. In fact, the more you humble yourself in His presence the greater your peace will be. Christian pride should not be in who we are as individuals but because His Spirit lives within us. That is a reason to be joyful!

As we humble ourselves, He lifts us up. He brings new meaning to each day that we live. You see, it is in Christ that we have a fullness of life and through Him that we are given the opportunity to be His vessels. Remember that it is in the brokenness of our spirit that we look and see His Spirit ready to serve us.

Commit Yourself

Do not be afraid to commit your life to Jesus Christ. He will not have you do anything that is out of God's perfect will for your life. There are many blessings that await you. Commitment to Christ means you care and want to be a complete Christian.

Commitment to Christ can be one of your greatest decisions. Christ has called you to be His own to follow His example. In taking on a total commitment to live for Christ, frustration is quickly defeated. As you give your life to Him, under the leadership of the Holy Spirit, your cup will be filled time and time again. Commitment to God is demonstrated by our attitudes and actions toward people. You can discover great joy in your life by sharing Christian love with others.

Commitment is a necessary part of the Christian life. If we don't fully commit ourselves to Jesus, we rob ourselves of many special moments with Him. It is in commitment to Him that He shows more of His holiness to us.

Trust

Trust Christ! Trust and believe that Christ can overcome frustration, hardships, pain, suffering, and any other forces that strike out at us.

Jesus will teach, direct, instruct, and in fact carry you through the tough times. Then Jesus will walk with you during the good ones too! Jesus will share all He has with you because He loves you.

When you trust Christ for everything, you are acknowledging that, "I know in whom I believe and there is nothing to fear. You are the One who is most concerned for my life, and I trust You completely." Trust does not happen overnight. It is a growing, continual relationship with the Savior. In the acknowledgment that you really do believe in Christ and understand what the gift of eternal life through Christ means, others see your faith in action.

Trusting Jesus is a way of saying, "I am Yours, do what You will! I believe that whatever You direct me to is best for me." When we learn to trust Christ, we tell Him that we know that He will do something special in our lives to draw us into a closer relationship with Him. We are, in fact, saying to the Lord, "I want whatever You have for me! I know God's best is available for me, and I accept it." Trusting is learning to follow. It is giving Christ the opportunity to make the most of our character.

Trusting Christ does not make you a robot or an unfeeling creature. It makes you God's person, one who is fully aware of the Holy Spirit within. The major promise which Christ has given us is for life eternal. As we take the gift of salvation for our very own, we are also accepting Christ's offerings to us. The Christ-led life is filled with promises and surprises. With each step taken in the knowledge and wisdom, the reality of being God's child becomes more and more important. There is no greater happiness, Christian friend, than being a part of God's Kingdom. There is no better life than the life that seeks to follow the pattern and examples left for us by Christ the Lord. It all comes in trusting and believing. Christ our Lord will never fail us. Salvation is ours for the taking by staking claims to it through total acceptance of Christ as Savior.

By trusting Christ for all things, we easily overcome the feelings frustration leaves within. Even when we have temporary setbacks, there is nothing that can fully separate us from Christ. We are His and He is ours.

After all is said and done, frustration has no value in life. It has no one to harm as we stand firm in Christ. Frustration is defeated. Look with me for a moment at some verses. "But thank God! He gives us victory through our Lord Jesus Christ. So, my dear brothers, continue to be firm, incapable of being moved, always letting the cup run over in the work of the Lord, because you know that your labor in the service of the Lord is never thrown away" (1 Corinthians 15:57, 58 Williams).

Then again in 1 Corinthians 16:13, 14, "Be on the alert, stand firm in the faith, act like men, be strong. Let all that you do be done in love" (NAS). The answer is before us and stands firm. We are to be strong through Christ the Lord. When we respond to others and look outside ourselves to share the love that is ours, there is no work frustration can do. For it is in sharing our love of Christ that we find meaning and purpose to life. Let us step forward, knowing where our security and trust lie—it is in Jesus.

QUESTIONS
1. List the steps we need to take in overcoming frustration in our lives.

2. How important is the proper relationship with Jesus Christ in defeating frustration?
   a. not at all important
   b. has some importance
   c. important
   d. very important
   e. vital

3. Which Scriptures tend to encourage you most in understanding frustration?

4. Who is able to overcome frustration easier—the nonbeliever or the believer in Christ? Why?

5. Describe the importance of understanding your relationship with Christ as Lord and Savior when problems beset you.

6. Why do we tend to forget that we need not be bothered by frustrations?

7. In what area of your life do you need Christ to help you the most?

8. Have you sought His divine guidance for each day of your life? Explain why or why not.

9. Now that you understand the steps to take in overcoming frustration, how will you put this information into practice in your life?

10. Make a list of persons you know who would be glad to gain new insight for dealing with the problem of frustration. Will you commit some of your time to sharing the ideas in this book with them?

chapter
7

a new tomorrow

*Faith in God makes a person
undaunted, unafraid, undivided,
and 'unflappable.'
Real faith results in active
response, responsive action, and
willing obedience.
Faith is continuing to run the race,
assured that you will get
your second wind.
Faith is focusing on God's
promises, and cropping out the
world's discouragements.
Faith is confidently expecting
miracles from the Source and
Promiser of miracles.*

William A. Ward

The subject of this chapter has so much to offer that I scarcely know where to begin. We will concentrate on the power of peace, the necessity of faith, and the joy of thinking positive thoughts. The chapter is dedicated to those of you who have already found peace and to those of you who have yet to claim the peace that is yours through Jesus Christ.

I haven't always run the race for Christ with my head held high. The fact is that for most of my life I never knew the race was even being run. When I learned that my life was involved in a marathon event that was being run by each of us, I saw my need to develop the right skills for living. It was not until I learned that I was not in competition with others that I found the race was not as difficult as I imagined.

Paul says, "Do you not know that in a race the runners all run, but only one can get the prize? You must run in such a way that you can get the prize. Any man who enters an athletic contest practices rigid self-control in training, only to win a wreath that withers, but we are in to win a wreath that never withers. So that is the way I run, with no uncertainty as to winning. That is the way I box, not like one that punches the air. But I keep on beating and bruising my body and making it my slave, so that I, after I have summoned others to the race, may not myself become unfit to run" (1 Corinthians 9:24–27 Williams).

The prize we gain for running a good race is a wreath of faith. Our faith will not wither as time passes by. It will only grow more beautiful. As we come to fullness of faith, we appreciate the value of a peaceful heart. Peace does not come quickly but is gained through experiences and trials. Peace is a symbol of belief, security, and full trust. The Christian who has not found peace has many anxious moments. Peace is necessary, for without it we face many moments of frustration. Peace in the soul quenches frustrations in the mind. Peace is the calmness of attitudes that lends security in even the strangest of circumstances.

Peace

The person who has not understood peace is tossed to and fro by all manner of problems. To gain peace over frustration is our goal. It is hoped that you have discovered it. Through our understanding of God's principles, knowing He has a designated plan for each individual life, we have learned how Christians can deal with frustration.

Let's take a few moments to look at God's Word, the Bible, to gain additional insight on the matter of peace. We will study individual verses and relate them to ourselves.

Psalm 4:6–8 says, "There are many who say, 'Who will show us any good?' Lord, lift up the light of Your countenance upon us. You have put gladness in my heart, more than in the season that their grain and wine increased. I will both lie down in peace, and sleep; for You alone, O Lord, make me dwell in safety" (NKJV). To understand the message of peace contained in these verses, let us think about what the writer is saying.

1. The psalmist says, "You have put gladness into my heart." Gladness is happiness. Happiness brings contentment, and contentment is a partner of peace. Gladness erases the sadness and gloom that seek to shadow the presence of God. Gladness in our spirit allows the light of the Son of God to shine through. Surely those of us who know Christ as the Prince of Peace have something to be glad about. The Lord Jesus Christ brings gladness to those who will accept Him and worship His holiness.

2. The person who lies down in peace must feel secure. A person who has fear in his or her heart finds it difficult to lie down. There is fear of the unknown and fear that perhaps an enemy is nearby waiting for the right moment to strike. As we see from the psalmist, not only will he lie down to rest in peace; he fully intends to sleep. In this time of sleep the psalmist gives us the impression that he knows he will rest peacefully.

Peace within the spirit allows us to rest in the assurance that God has control of each situation. We need not sleep with one eye open, so to speak, but we can sleep knowing that we are secure in the love of our Lord. Peace removes doubt and anxiousness from our spirit and replaces them with a calm assurance.

Christian friend, our trust in Christ will give us perfect peace. It will allow us to function within the safeguards that Christ has established for us. How, then, is peace given us? Why, through Christ our Lord and Savior, of course! It is a gift from Him. It is ours as we give away those anxious moments and believe that the Holy Spirit will act as our Protector. Let us look at some of the words Jesus spoke on the subject of peace.

Turn to John 14:25–29. Recall the scene: Jesus is speaking with the disciples. He has told them that He is going away. "I have told you this while I am still staying with you. But the Helper, the Holy Spirit, whom the Father will send to represent me, will teach you everything Himself, and cause you to remember everything that I have told you. I now leave you the blessing of peace, I give you the blessing of my own peace. I myself do not give it in the way the world gives it. Stop letting your hearts be troubled or timid. You have heard me say that I am going away and coming back to you; if you really love me, you would rejoice over my telling you that I am going to the Father, because my Father is greater than I. And now I have told you this before it takes place, that when it does take place you may believe in me" (Williams).

This Scripture speaks to us in a manner as meaningful today as when Jesus first spoke it. Read it again as though Jesus were talking to you.

1. "I am leaving you [speak your name here], the blessing of peace." "Why would you want to do that for me, Jesus?" you might ask. Because of His great love for you. A blessing of peace from Christ cannot be stolen away from you. It is a gift that is yours because of His perfect and holy life. He gives it to you because He does not want your life to be lived on uncertain ground. In the blessing of peace there is confidence.

2. "I give you the blessings of my own peace." Jesus, God's Son, stands before you and offers you a blessing of peace for the rest of your life. He even gives you the full assurance of the Holy Spirit, who will come and take His place so that you will not have to endure alone.

3. With the blessing of peace and the guidance of the Holy Spirit to teach each Christian, there is no force that can overpower us. Accepting the gift that Jesus has given us allows us to have a peace that surpasses all human understanding. The world cannot measure the peace that has been given you in human terms, for it is beyond human comprehension. The blessing of peace that comes from Jesus is a partial measure of His love for us. Christ's peace is the reassurance that even in giving His all for us there is still more. Peace is a most precious gift.

Peace beyond measure can belong to the child of God. We have the blessed assurance that the Lord is concerned about every detail of our lives. The moments that have been the most frustrating need not remain that way for those who love the Lord God. It is in these worrisome moments that God often allows His Spirit of peace to take control of the situation. Instead of chaos there is often a calmness. We are called to live a peaceful life as seen in Psalm 34:14: "Depart from evil, and do good; seek peace, and pursue it" (NKJV).

Peace is the result of a calm spirit. Peace is feeling certain and secure in a given situation although everything about us seems to be falling apart. The contentment that Christ brings to our lives cannot be measured in lengths and breadths but in completeness. You see, Christian friend, the tranquility of Christ is ours because He proves Himself faithful time and time again. Thus we learn to trust Him more and more in times of trial, for it is Christ who changes lives and situations. It is Christ who takes our unlovely parts and transforms us into a beautiful vessel.

Peace through every situation is ours when we share our lives with Him. His way is reliable, and He has shown us that He is loyal at all times. Christ at the head of the life of each individual member of the body of Christ brings incredible results. When we entrust Christ with all areas of our lives, we gain the fruit of the Spirit as a part of our relationship with Him. Just to remind you, "the fruit of the Spirit is love, joy, peace, longsuffering, kindness, goodness, faithfulness, gentleness, self-control" (Galatians 5:22, 23a NKJV).

Each new tomorrow can be filled with these attitudes as we allow the Spirit to reap the harvest that is sown as we grow in the knowledge of Christ. These qualities become a real part of our spirit, for in our association with Christ as Lord and Savior each of the qualities is learned through experiencing life and growing in faith.

I hope this view on peace is not new to you. Possibly you have applied it to your life for years. But then there are those who are learning its value for the first time. If you are a newcomer to this view, remember that gaining peace is just the starting point. There is far more to our Christian way of life than just receiving peace. When the peace of Jesus Christ comes into our lives, then we are prepared to serve in other areas of life. Peace is a stepping stone across the stream of life. With each step the way becomes surer, and we find ourselves ready to experience still another joy in our Christian walk.

THE LORD OF PEACE

"But now through your union with Christ Jesus you who were once far away have through the blood of Christ been brought near. For He Himself is our peace, He is the one who has made us both into one body and has broken down the barrier that kept us apart; through His human nature He has put a stop to the hostility between us, namely, the law with its commands and decrees, in order to create one new humanity out of the two parties and so make peace through union with Himself, and in one body to reconcile them both to God with His cross after He had killed the hostility through it. When He came, He brought the good news of peace for you who were far away and for you who were near; for it is by Him through one Spirit that both of us now have an introduction to the Father. So you are no longer foreigners and strangers, but you are fellow citizens of God's people and members of His family; for you are built upon the foundation of the apostles and prophets, with Christ Jesus Himself the cornerstone. In union with Him the whole building is harmoniously fitted together and continues to grow into a temple, sacred through its union with the Lord, and you yourselves, in union with Him, in fellowship with one another, are being built up into a dwelling for God through the Spirit" (Ephesians 2:13–22 Williams).

This passage gives us an abundance of information about our Lord.

1. He is our peace.
2. Through Him we can achieve peace through perfect unity.
3. He has given us a better way to live—filled with peace, contentment, happiness, with a purpose to live.
4. He has brought us the good news that we are no longer foreigners to the family of God but a part of Him. As our Savior has given us a better way to live, we are to accept it and build upon it.
5. Christ is the cornerstone of faith. With Christ as the cornerstone, we build our lives on a foundation that will not crumble and fall.
6. We are part of His work. Each Christian is part of the whole building (the true church—the body of believers). Perhaps some of us stand a little stronger than the others, but each of us is vital.
7. Through Christ we have fellowship with one another. This is to say that wherever there are Christian people, then we are to share fellowship and love. Through our communication and sharing with one another, we are encouraged and enlightened. The Lord will be present among us. He is a part of the lives of all believers.

There is such a blessing to being a member of the family of Christ. We are continually in communication with others who share our faith in Christ. Christ gives us a "newness of life." We have a bond of love in the unity of the Lord. There is something special about this bond that my meager words cannot describe. It is the security that faith and trust in Christ give. When we are with other Christian men and women, there should be an attitude of trust. We are to build with one another as we have opportunity to share our faith.

Christ as the Lord of our lives brings a peace that is certain and pure. The light of His love grows brighter each day. The closer we draw to Him, the more brilliant the light, until one day we will stand in His glorious presence.

"And may the Lord who gives us peace give you peace in whatever circumstances you may be. The Lord be with you all." (2 Thessalonians 3:16 Williams). What wonderful words of cheer! The Lord does give peace in whatever circumstances you may be in. He will give it. He seeks to give it. Whatever situation you are walking through right this moment, yes, *right now,* there is peace available to you.

Perhaps you do have the Lord's peace and are resting in complete faith and trust in Him. However, many Christians do not feel God's peace. Are you one of them? His peace is available, Christian friend. You need only ask for it, and it is given. Frustration, worry, anger, anxiety, grief, strife, and loss of purpose are all overcome through the love of Christ. He can tend to anything! The key to overcoming is before you in the name of Jesus the Lord. Allow Him to be more than a name to call on in time of hardship. Allow Him to guide you through the good times and the bad, for He has your best interests in mind.

Love

It would be impossible to face a new tomorrow without learning how to live today. Love is such a valuable gift to give another person. The Christian who has his or her life "altogether" cannot resist an opportunity to share love. Love is a natural part of the Christ-led life. For it is in Christ that we know love, and it is because of what He has taught us that we can share it.

To love and be loved are a natural part of life. The Christian who does not love must take a close look at his or her life. Christ desires us to love others through His expression of love for us. If we don't love others, something is not in proper perspective in our life.

Love is more than a feeling or an attitude. For the Christian, it is to be a way of life. Loving others through the love of Christ is a must for the believer. Time and time again we are instructed on the importance of loving others. Meaningful teachings and thoughtful encouragement are found in the Scripture passages concerning love. Yet many Christians ignore their responsibility to love one another as Christ has loved them.

With each new day there is a challenge to love one another with the love of Christ. A pure, unselfish, genuine love that comes from God is ours to give. When we keep it for ourselves and selfishly resist His command to love, we rob our lives of a beautiful blessing and a wonderful opportunity to share Christ.

Turn with me to 1 John 4:7–12, and let's read the Word of God together. "Dear friends, let us love one another, for love comes from God. Everyone who loves has been born of God and knows God. Whoever does not love does not know God, because God is love. This is how God showed his love among us: He sent his one and only Son into the world that we might live through him. This is love: not that we loved God, but that he loved us and sent his Son as an atoning sacrifice for our sins. Dear friends, since God so loved us, we also ought to love one another. No one has ever seen God; but if we love each other, God lives in us and his love is made complete in us" (NIV).

How beautiful are these words of 1 John. Their truth is everlasting. Throughout the ages men and women have read these words and applied them to their lives. Ask yourself, "Have I allowed the words in these verses to speak to my heart? Do I believe they are true? Do I allow God's Word to motivate my life in a manner that will display His love in my life?" It is very important that Christians understand the teachings on the subject of love.

To refuse to love is to say that we do not know God. I know that may be tough to deal with, but we must. The person who lacks a loving spirit in the new life Christ gives is not living for Christ. For, you see, Jesus taught that love is the key to life. Jesus came to love and to show us love at its greatest level by sacrificing His life for our sins. This is the basis of love as seen in the eyes of God.

Look at what the Scripture teaches: "Whoever does not love does not know God, because God is love" (1 John 4:8 NKJV). To reject the opportunity to love another in Christlike love is to turn away from God. None of us who have experienced Christ as Lord and Savior would want to willingly turn away from His love. Life is made worth living because Jesus is a part of our spirit.

Let's read once again from the same passage in 1 John, "No one has ever seen God; but if we love each other, God lives in us and his love is made complete in us." The only comment necessary at this point is that we should give grateful praise to God for His involvement in our lives. God's love is made complete in us by our willingness to respond to His call. God, like love, cannot be self-contained but must be shared, so that we can be fulfilled and abundantly blessed.

If you think this subject is a sore spot to me, then you are correct. Very often there are people who are highly respected in the Christian community. They tell us we should do this and be that as we serve the Lord with gladness. They tell us about the power we have in our lives because we are children of God. They challenge us to be bold and call forth the powers of God that we might share the faith. On and on they go. They seemingly have wonderful insight and have mastered the teachings of the Scriptures, but yet they may be lacking in one area— love. It has been my observation that many of the men and women who expound upon the Scriptures to lead us to the truth of God avoid teaching on the necessity of love within the heart of the believer.

Throughout many crusades, revivals, and sermons it has become obvious that many of our speakers avoid the subject of godly love toward one another. They bring to mind the need for the message in 1 Corinthians 13:1: "If I speak in the tongues of men and of angels, but have not love, I am only a resounding gong or a clanging cymbal" (NIV). They make loud noises proclaiming the truth of God's Word, and yet there is no visible sign of love in their lives. It troubles me that our messengers seem more intent on a message that states, "If you do not do this . . . such and such will happen. Those aren't my words, they are God's. Don't blame me! I am only God's messenger." The messenger, whether a minister or lay person, who speaks to us in this manner should make an evaluation of his or her life. It appears they are far more interested in displaying the person they think they are and the person they wish us to be instead of the teachers of the "Good News."

When a person speaks to us using this slanted approach, we must surely wonder what it is they are trying to prove? Surely there is no indication of humbleness, for there seems to be none reflected in this approach; nor is there any love, for their message comes across as a threat instead of a challenge. Without love, even the best speaker makes nothing but noise. Love is not self-seeking or boastful. Love is gentle, kind, giving, forgiving, open, genuine, truthful, compassionate, and warm.

Love is God speaking within us. He tells us to love in a way so that *He* will be seen in your life. Love is quiet and well-mannered, not firmly rooted in pride and selfish ego. In living our lives for God there is no need to make sounds like the wind blowing through the trees. Instead we should quietly demonstrate the rippling effect that God's love has had on our lives and allow it to gently spread to others.

Love does not threaten. It does not say, "Do it my way because my way is best." Love leads to encouragement. Love allows others to desire to grow in the Christlike love that is set before them. Love is God within us, allowing us to be a part of His work as we walk with Him each day.

Once again let's read from 1 John 4:18–21: "There is no fear in love. But perfect love drives out fear, because fear has to do with punishment. The man who fears is not made perfect in love. We love because He first loved us. If anyone says, 'I love God,' and yet hates his brother, he is a liar. For anyone who does not love his brother, whom he has seen, cannot love God, whom he has not seen. And He has given us this command: Whoever loves God must also love his brother" (NIV).

Throughout the world there are many people who are afraid to love. I know this to be true and I expect you do too. At one time in my life I had this experience. Please allow me to express some of my ideas about why people are afraid to love. As we expose these attitudes and feelings, others may come to your mind. Make a list of them in your notebook for reference. It is in looking at our fears that we can overcome them. There may be someone who needs your guidance and love to overcome the fear that keeps them from loving.

1. Often people are afraid to love because they fear rejection. Offering your Christian love to another and having it thrown back in your face isn't much fun. Rejection of your love hurts! It is difficult to understand why anyone refuses love, but they do. It has happened to me when I have offered Christian love, and it will happen to you. But we must continue to love regardless and allow the Holy Spirit to achieve whatever purpose He desires through your love.

2. People may be afraid to love because they lack commitment. To love another takes effort. It takes the desire to become a part of that person's life. In our Christian walk the degree of involvement may be great or small, depending on what our Lord has planned. Commitment takes time, dedication, effort, and concern. Frankly, there are many people who are unwilling to commit even a part of their lives to the work of the Lord.

3. Involvement is saying, "I care about you. I want to help you if there is something I can do. Allow me to do this for you. I will pray for you each day." Each of these ideas carries concern and love as banners that say, "I love you." Being concerned for others means there is a need to share your life. It goes hand in hand with commitment. Involvement in loving someone is saying, "I think you are important not only to God but to me."

4. There are people who are afraid to love others, because they do not want to share with others. This may involve sharing of your earthly treasures, your spiritual gifts, your talents, or your life in general. People who cannot love with the love of Christ are tied down by the ropes of selfishness. Only as you release your life from this bondage will you experience the joy of the Christian walk.

The Christian who has learned the value of loving others is a "tool" of the Lord. As others see the love of Christ within the Christian, they see something that is desirable and worthwhile. If they do not find the love of Christ, they may steer clear of you even though they may be drawn to you in a strange sort of way. They may not like you as a person, but they may want what you have. It is especially true in the family of Christ that those who have not learned to give love avoid those who share love.

The love we offer as Christians displays our concerns for others from the Holy Spirit's view, not our own. Frequently, those we want to love the most are the ones we feel are the least lovable. Their continual rejection of our love nevertheless causes them concern. They don't love us, but yet there is something about us that draws them toward godly love. They will, in time, have to deal with their responsibility to love through Christ.

For those who accept the love of Christ and love in return there is harmony and peace. How exciting and beautiful to love another Christian and have it returned. We can enjoy our expression of concern and love as we share our faith in Christ. Ours is not a "mushy" or "sticky" love. It is a love that says, "I love you in the Lord. I am concerned for you and have you in my heart. You share Christ's love with me through our bond of salvation in Jesus Christ."

There just isn't enough said about the warmth a Christian friend lends to our heart. Strength and courage are found through the sharing of Christ. There is security and peace to share. There is rejoicing in gladness and weeping in our sorrow as we share our lives with Christian friends. Each new tomorrow only makes our bond of love and friendship stronger, for we share our lives and our faith through a daily walk with Christ. I love my Christian friends very greatly, for they are my encouragers, my prayer partners, my strength when I need support, my fellow servants in the family of Christ. They are ever so important to me regardless of my involvement with them on a regular basis, for it is through them that I share fellowship and love. Our bond is Christ. He makes us stronger and more useable as we share love through Him.

Yes, love is the key. It is spread in numerous ways to all people. But it is nothing until we share it. It is a tool used to draw us closer to God by sharing with others. It is a blessing and a joy to share God's love wherever we may go.

Joy

As we learn to overcome frustration and step forth with a renewed spirit, we will surely experience joy in our lives. The joy encountered among Christians is not the same expression of joy that the world encounters. It is a joy that is often inexpressible, and yet we are filled with a feeling that gives us reason to rejoice in our Lord Jesus Christ.

Joy is a form of happiness. There have been moments when I have seen something special accomplished in the life of another Christian (or even in my own life) and have felt almost overcome by joy. Writing has brought unmeasured joy to my spirit. It has allowed me to be filled with a spirit of excitement and contentment.

Joy is a gift from God given us as a reward. It allows us to express our gladness. While nonbelievers often feel that Christians never have any fun or enjoyment in life, they tend to be baffled when they encounter our exuberance when something special occurs in our life. They do not understand why we feel cheerful and in awe when the Lord gives us one of those special moments to cherish. Joy comes in being a part of God's work and in seeing results come. Joy is a blessing all its own. As we learn to focus our lives on Christ, we begin to see more reasons to be glad.

Joy gives pleasure because it is a result of being a part of something and seeing what God has done through the effort. Frustration has no opportunity to creep in when joy is present. With a renewed mind which focuses on Christ, there is the opportunity to experience even greater joy. For the Christian man or woman there is a reason to rejoice in everything. Philippians 4:4, 5 says it well: "Rejoice in the Lord always. I will say it again: Rejoice! Let your gentleness be evident to all. The Lord is near" (NIV).

The Lord is indeed near. We have a reason to be glad. We should live our lives rejoicing in the knowledge of this Scripture alone. We have no reason to fear anything. Nothing need overcome us, especially now that we understand what steps to take in dealing with frustration, for the Lord is near. We have to claim our joys and rejoice in the knowledge that the Holy Spirit is a part of our Christian lives. Christians, let's start living in the positive and put aside the frustrations of life. Today is a new day, let's use it to glorify the work of Jesus Christ.

Knowledge

Our newly gained knowledge in dealing with frustration should surely lift our spirits. It does, after all, take all the fear and frustration that seek to overshadow us and puts them away from us. Let's look at some Scriptures on the subject of knowledge and its importance in the Christian life.

Proverbs 24:5 says, "A wise man has great power, and a man of knowledge increases strength" (NIV). To gain knowledge takes effort. We must want to learn. This can be applied to all areas of life, but since we are speaking of spiritual matters we will concentrate on this area of life. Knowledge is found through studying, experiencing, and living the Word of God in our heart. The more receptive we are to the teachings and guidance of the Holy Spirit, the more we learn.

It is through seeking to know God that we truly find Him. How often have you heard someone say, "I really wish I had time to read the Bible, but there are so many other things I would rather do"? This excuse is shallow, for the person who really wants to learn what the Scriptures teach can make time to read the Bible. I grew up in an era before most of the modern Bible translations were available. The restlessness I felt from wanting to understand the King James Version of the Bible only drove me further away from God's Word. My excuse was that all those thee's, thou's, and therefore's were difficult to understand.

It was not until the *Living Bible* was marketed that I found the solution to my problem. I had not known various translations of the Bible were available. As I began to read from the *Living Bible,* I could not get enough information in my head. I wanted more. Within a few months it was time for me to move to another translation. Then I went to another and yet another, so that I might learn the teachings of the Scriptures in depth.

We live in an age that is filled with technical advances. There is a vast amount of information in the form of commentaries, various translations of the Bible, workbooks, study courses, and, of course, books on various subjects of interest to those who desire to gain more knowledge on a given subject. Perhaps more than at any other time in history, there are more resources available to give us insight on various subjects and teachings of the Scriptures. We no longer have the excuse, "I can't understand what the Bible says." Anyone who reads the Word of God will come away with some information.

To know what the Bible teaches is to desire to learn. There must be a starting point. We must make an effort to read the Scriptures for ourselves to discover the message God has given us. Knowledge is gained through desire to know God better. To improve our relationship and understanding of the Father, we must read His Instruction Book for life. Many things that seem to be mysteries are answered when we seek to know God's Word.

There are some beautiful teachings in the Bible. They were written for you and me. They were written for those yet to be born. They were written for the Christians in the early Church. The Bible should be honored as a blessing sent for those who seek to understand God's instruction. For it is a book that is timeless and meaningful. The teachings of Paul, Peter, John, Matthew, Luke, and Mark are as true today as they were the day the Holy Spirit inspired them to write. We ought to be glad the information of the Scriptures is available to us. We ought to understand the necessity of growing in knowledge and wisdom each day and be glad that God has given us the Word to lend us strength. The Christian who will truly seek to know God will not be disappointed, for He will respond to his or her efforts.

Wisdom

Wisdom is a precious gift given to those who are deserving of it. It seems that wisdom is a much sought after gift. The person who gains wisdom has a special blessing from God. It is a gift that enables the receiver to work through problems with a certain insight that is most admirable. The person who has wisdom gives guidance and understanding of situations to those who do not have it.

There is an opportunity for each of us to gain wisdom. As we learn to deal with frustration, worry, struggle, pain, suffering, and a host of other difficulties, wisdom is gained. Each new tomorrow will allow us to gain a certain amount of wisdom, for our situations are continually changing. In this section of our study, let's learn the value of wisdom in our lives. Wisdom is important to the Christian life, for with it we maintain a proper balance in our walk with the Lord.

Colossians 1:9, 10 says, "For this reason, since that day we heard about you, we have not stopped praying for you and asking God to fill you with the knowledge of His will through all spiritual wisdom and understanding. And we pray this in order that you may live a life worthy of the Lord and may please Him in every way: bearing fruit in every good work, growing in the knowledge of God" (NIV).

Wisdom is an important gift that is to be appreciated and used under the direction of God. You might ask, "How important is wisdom to the Christian life?" The answer lies in the words of Proverbs 4:5–7:

"Get wisdom! Get understanding! Do not forget, nor turn away from the words of my mouth. Do not forsake her, and she will preserve you; Love her, and she will keep you. Wisdom is the principal thing; Therefore get wisdom. And in all your getting, get understanding" (NKJV).

Proverbs 8 fully instructs us on the importance of wisdom and the excellence it provides in our lives. Proverbs 9:1–12 gives us the ways of wisdom. Bear in mind that wisdom, like any other gift, is ours because of Christ. We are to gain wisdom and use it in a manner that will glorify God, for it is in gaining the understanding of things through the Spirit's teachings that we can deal with the adversities of life.

Dealing with frustration has not been easy. It has taken effort on our part. We have had to deal with changes to establish a new and better way of life. Learning to deal with frustration through the Holy Spirit has led us to a deeper understanding of Christ's total concern for our lives, for it has been by the Spirit's guidance that we have been victors over frustration in our lives.

You must now take the information you have learned and use it. Not to do so would allow the enemy to creep in and bother you again. Study the Word, apply it to your heart, pray for guidance, and listen as the Holy Spirit speaks to your heart. Learn to be God's complete person through the blessings that are yours in Jesus Christ the Lord.

QUESTIONS
1. What is the most important information that you learned in Psalm 4?

2. How can it be applied to your life?

3. What confidence do Christians have through the Holy Spirit in their lives?

4. Why is an understanding of the work of the Holy Spirit important to the Christian?

5. Do those who do not believe in Christ as Lord and Savior have this same confidence? Read John 14:25–29.

6. In your own words describe the blessings of peace that belong to us through Christ.

7. How does peace contribute to a happy spirit?

8. Reread Ephesians 2:13–22. How are these verses important to each Christian?

9. What do you believe Christian love is?

10. Describe a person you know who has not grasped the importance of love as taught by Christ. What needs do you see in his or her life? How is he or she different from persons who allow the love of Christ to flow freely in their lives?

11. Why is godly love an important quality in the life of the believer?

12. Read 1 John 4:7–12. How do these verses affect your thinking on the importance of love as a Christian?

13. How do we learn to experience joy as we overthrow the frustrations that we encounter?

14. How important is joy to you at this point in time? Why?

15. What knowledge is gained through a personal commitment to Christ?

16. How do we gain knowledge to deal with life's problems?

17. What is the importance of wisdom in the Christian life?

18. How is wisdom gained?

19. Locate and write three verses that speak of the importance of wisdom in your life.

20. Why is wisdom a desirable spiritual gift?

21. How can you share the wisdom and insight you gain from God?

22. What are the steps used to deal with frustration? (Think about the previous chapters and recall each step.)

chapter
8

scriptures of encouragement

These scriptures are placed at the end of our study to benefit you, the reader, and to encourage you. Whenever you feel let down or your burdens seem heaviest, turn to this section. Read these passages from the Word of God, and allow them to speak to your heart. Your burdens will seem lighter.

1. "He who raised the Lord Jesus will raise us also with Jesus and will present us with you" (2 Corinthians 4:14 NAS).

2. "Not that we are adequate in ourselves to consider anything as coming from ourselves, but our adequacy is from God" (2 Corinthians 3:5 NAS).

3. "There is therefore now no condemnation to those who are in Christ Jesus, who do not walk according to the flesh but according to the Spirit" (Romans 8:1 NKJV).

4. "Let love be without hypocrisy. Abhor what is evil. Cling to what is good. Be kindly affectionate to one another with brotherly love, in honor giving preference to one another; not lagging in diligence, fervent in spirit, serving the Lord; rejoicing in hope, patient in tribulation, continuing steadfastly in prayer" (Romans 12:9–12 NKJV).

5. "Love does no harm to a neighbor; therefore love is the fulfillment of the law" (Romans 13:10 NKJV).

6. "You, however, are controlled not by the sinful nature but by the Spirit, if the Spirit of God lives in you. And if anyone does not have the Spirit of Christ, he does not belong to Christ. But if Christ is in you, your body is dead because of sin, yet your spirit is alive because of righteousness" (Romans 8:9,10 NIV).

7. "If anyone suffers as a Christian, let him not feel ashamed, but in that name let him glorify God" (1 Peter 4:16 NAS).

8. "Humble yourselves, therefore, under the mighty hand of God, that He may exalt you at the proper time" (1 Peter 5:6 NAS).

9. "Whoever does not love has never come to know God by experience, because God is love" (1 John 4:8 Williams).

10. "God is love, and whoever continues to love continues in union with God and God in union with him. Our love attains perfection through our having perfect confidence about the day of judgment, because here in this world we are living as He did" (1 John 4:16b, 17 Williams).

11. "See what wonderful love the Father has bestowed on us in letting us be called God's children, and that is what we are! This is why the world does not know what we are, because it has never come to know Him" (1 John 3:1 Williams).

12. "I have been crucified with Christ, so that I myself no longer live, but Christ is living in me; the life I now live as a mortal man I live by faith in the Son of God who loved me and gave Himself for me. I never can nullify the unmerited favor of God. For if right standing with God could come through law, then Christ died for nothing" (Galatians 2:20, 21 Williams).

13. "I mean this: Practice living by the Spirit and then by no means will you gratify the cravings of your lower nature. For the cravings of the lower nature are just the opposite to those of the Spirit, and the cravings of the Spirit are just the opposite of those of the lower nature; these two are opposed to each other, so that you cannot do anything you please" (Galatians 5:16, 17 Williams).

14. "Grow in the grace and knowledge of our Lord and Savior Jesus Christ. To Him be the glory, both now and to the day of eternity. Amen" (2 Peter 3:18 NAS).

15. "Do not marvel, brethren, if the world hates you" (1 John 3:13 NAS).

16. "In this is love, not that we loved God, but that He loved us and sent His Son to be the propitiation for our sins. Beloved, if God so loved us, we also ought to love one another" (1 John 4:10, 11 NAS).

17. "He has regarded the prayer of the destitute, and has not despised their prayer" (Psalm 102:17 NAS).

18. "Let the glory of the Lord endure forever; let the Lord be glad in His works" (Psalm 104:31 NAS).

19. "But the lovingkindness of the Lord is from everlasting to everlasting on those who fear Him" (Psalm 103:17a NAS).

20. "Teach me Thy way, O Lord; I will walk in Thy truth; unite my heart to fear Thy name. I will give thanks to Thee, O Lord my God, with all my heart, and will glorify Thy name forever" (Psalm 86:11, 12 NAS).

21. " 'I love thee, O Lord, my strength.' The Lord is my rock and my fortress and my deliverer, My God, my rock, in whom I take refuge; my shield and the horn of my salvation, my stronghold" (Psalm 18:1, 2 NAS).

22. "There is no wisdom or understanding or counsel against the Lord" (Proverbs 21:30 NKJV).

23. "Do not speak in the hearing of a fool, for he will despise the wisdom of your words" (Proverbs 23:9 NKJV).

24. "Son, be of good cheer; your sins are forgiven you" (Matthew 9:2b NKJV).

25. "Do not fear therefore; you are of more value than many sparrows" (Matthew 10:31 NKJV).

26. "When anyone hears the word of the kingdom, and does not understand it, then the wicked one comes and snatches away what was sown in his heart" (Matthew 13:19a, b NKJV).

27. "A good man out of the good treasure of his heart brings forth good things, and an evil man out of the evil treasure brings forth evil things" (Matthew 12:35 NKJV).

28. "Be of good cheer! It is I; do not be afraid" (Matthew 14:27b NKJV).

29. "Therefore take heed that the light which is in you is not darkness. If then your whole body is full of light, having no part dark, the whole body will be full of light, as when the bright shining of a lamp gives you light" (Luke 11:35, 36 NKJV).

30. "So the Lord said, 'If you have faith as a mustard seed, you can say to this mulberry tree, "Be pulled up by the roots and be planted in the sea," and it would obey you' " (Luke 17:6 NKJV).

31. "Whoever seeks to save his life will lose it, and whoever loses his life will preserve it" (Luke 17:33 NKJV).

32. "Jesus replied: ' "Love the Lord your God with all your heart and with all your soul and with all your mind." This is the first and greatest commandment. And the second is like it: "Love your neighbor as yourself." All the Law and the Prophets hang on these two commandments' " (Matthew 22:37–40 NIV).

33. "The greatest among you will be your servant. For whoever exalts himself will be humbled, and whoever humbles himself will be exalted" (Matthew 23:11, 12 NIV).

34. " 'Come, follow me,' Jesus said, 'and I will make you fishers of men' " (Mark 1:17 NIV).

35. "The disciples were amazed at his words. But Jesus said again, 'Children, how hard it is to enter the kingdom of God! It is easier for a camel to go through the eye of a needle than for a rich man to enter the kingdom of God' " (Mark 10:24, 25 NIV).

36. "Consider how the lilies grow. They do not labor or spin. Yet I tell you, not even Solomon in all his splendor was dressed like one of these. If that is how God clothes the grass of the field, which is here today, and tomorrow is thrown into the fire, how much more will he clothe you, O you of little faith!" (Luke 12:27, 28 NIV).

37. " 'Peace be with you! As the Father has sent me, I am sending you.' And with that he breathed on them and said, 'Receive the Holy Spirit. If you forgive anyone his sins, they are forgiven; if you do not forgive them, they are not forgiven' " (John 20:21b–23 NIV).

38. "Three times I pleaded with the Lord to take it away from me. But he said to me, 'My grace is sufficient for you, for my power is made perfect in weakness' " (2 Corinthians 12:8, 9 NIV).

39. "For he himself is our peace, who has made the two one and has destroyed the barrier, the dividing wall of hostility, by abolishing in his flesh the law with its commandments and regulations. His purpose was to create in himself one new man out of the two, thus making peace, and in this one body to reconcile both of them to God through the cross, by which he put to death their hostility" (Ephesians 2:14–16 NIV).

40. "I became a servant of this gospel by the gift of God's grace given me through the working of his power" (Ephesians 3:7 NIV).

41. "And this is my prayer: that your love may abound more and more in knowledge and depth of insight, so that you may be able to discern what is best and may be pure and blameless until the day of Christ, filled with the fruit of righteousness that comes through Jesus Christ—to the glory and praise of God" (Philippians 1:9–11 NIV).

42. "Peace to the brothers, and love with faith from God the Father and the Lord Jesus Christ. Grace to all who love our Lord Jesus Christ with an undying love" (Ephesians 6:23, 24 NIV).

43. "May God himself, the God of peace, sanctify you through and through. May your whole spirit, soul and body be kept blameless at the coming of our Lord Jesus Christ. The one who calls you is faithful and he will do it" (1 Thessalonians 5:23, 24 NIV).

44. "May the Lord make your love increase and overflow for each other and for everyone else, just as ours does for you" (1 Thessalonians 3:12 NIV).

45. "For God did not appoint us to suffer wrath but to receive salvation through our Lord Jesus Christ" (1 Thessalonians 5:9 NIV).

46. "Once you were alienated from God and were enemies in your minds because of your evil behavior. But now he has reconciled you by Christ's physical body through death to present you holy in his sight, without blemish and free from accusation—if you continue in your faith, established and firm, not moved from the hope held out in the gospel" (Colossians 1:21–23a NIV).

47. "I pray that you may be active in sharing your faith, so that you will have a full understanding of every good thing we have in Christ" (Philemon 6 NIV).

48. "But the wisdom that comes from heaven is first of all pure; then peace loving, considerate, submissive, full of mercy and good fruit, impartial and sincere" (James 3:17 NIV).

49. "Faith by itself, if it is not accompanied by action, is dead" (James 2:17b, c NIV).

50. "Submit yourselves, then, to God. Resist the devil, and he will flee from you. Come near to God and he will come near to you" (James 4:7, 8a NIV).

index